SPEED WRITE
YOUR FIRST BOOK

Also by Mark Victor Hansen

BOOKS

Chicken Soup for the Soul series—254 different books in print

The One Minute Millionaire

Cracking the Millionaire Code

Cash in a Flash

How to Make the Rest of Your Life the Best of Your Life

The Aladdin Factor

Dare to Win

The Richest Kids in America

The Miracle of Tithing

The Power of Focus

The Miracles in You

Out of the Blue

Master Motivator

You Are the Solution

You Have a Book in You

Speed Write Your Personal Life Story

Speed Write Your First Fiction Book

Speed Write Your Nonfiction Book

Speed Write Your Mega Book Marketing Plan

Speed Write Your First Screenplay

Speed Write (and Deliver) Your Killer Speech

Speed Write Your Amazing Publishing Plan

Speed Edit Your First Book

Visualizing Is Realizing

Dreams Don't Have Deadlines

AUDIOS

How to Think Bigger than You Ever Thought You Could Think

Dreams Don't Have Deadlines

Visualizing Is Realizing

Sell Yourself Rich

Chicken Soup for the Soul series

The One Minute Millionaire

Cracking the Millionaire Code

SPEED WRITE YOUR FIRST BOOK

From Blank Spaces
to Great Pages
in Just 90 Days

MARK VICTOR HANSEN
AND STEVE GOTTRY

MEDIA

Published 2020 by Gildan Media LLC
aka G&D Media
www.GandDmedia.com

Front Cover design by David Rheinhardt of Pyrographx

Interior design by Meghan Day Healey of Story Horse, LLC

Library of Congress Cataloging-in-Publication Data is available upon request

ISBN: 978-1-7225-0329-1

10   9   8   7   6   5   4   3   2   1

Contents

Chapter One

Write Your Book in 90 Days! 11

How to Use This Book... 12

First Step: Gather Your Writing Tools.................................. 13

The FANAFI Principle 14

Fill in the Blanks! 15

The Four Considerations.. 16

Your Title Is Everything 17

Creating the Perfect Title Is Hard Work 19

Get a Website.. 20

Let's Get Started!... 20

Test, Test, Test!... 21

Choose a Literary Style 22

Chapter Two

The Essentials of Storytelling 25

Exercise Your Mind 26

Story and Character Development 27

What Is a Story? 27

The Four Cornerstones of Character Development 28

What Is Your Core Concept? 30

Avoid the Deus ex Machina 32

More on Character—Much More 33

The First Key to Developing Interesting Characters:
    Temperament Types 33

The Second Key to Character: Backstory 34

The Third Key to Character: Compelling Desire 35

Compelling Desires in Film and Literature 36

Here's the Big One: Critical Flaws! 37

Structure 39

Story Development 51

Understanding Power and Control 52

Understanding Conflict 53

The Roles of Characters 54

Suspension of Disbelief 56

Chapter Three

Let's Get Down to Business 59

Your Most Difficult Assignment.. 59

You're Ready to Write!... 78

Track Your Time 78

The First 30 Days.. 79

Days 31 to 60.. 80

Days 61 to 90.. 81

How Is It Going?.. 82

Honing Your Writing Skills: Tips to Live By 82

Don't Repeat Words.. 83

Think and Write in Threes... 84

Finish the Phrase and Get It Right: Grammar 101 84

Tips and Tricks from the Professionals 87

Use Power Words.. 88

Say It in Fresh Ways 89

Writing with Power.. 91

How to Achieve These Objectives... 92

Core Principles for Nonfiction Writers 92

Writing Books That Sell.. 93

Key Characteristics of a Successful Book................................. 93

Editing Your Work... 96

Rewriting: Painful, but Worth It!... 97

Grabbing Attention: The First Five 97

So Let's Do This Now!... 99

Chapter Four

Now That It's Finished 109

Feedback: The Breakfast of Champions 109

Copyrighting Your Work 110

Getting That Silly Bar Code 112

Publishing Your Book 112

Promoting Your Book 113

Other Promotional Tips 114

Software Resources 114

Book Proposal Guides 117

Additional Resources 117

Online and Related Resources 121

Acknowledgments 123

About the Authors 125

When you fill in the blanks . . .

*. . . you fill in the empty spaces and places
in the lives of your readers.*

Where there is numbing sameness,
you bring abundant variety.

Where adventure is missing,
you create exciting journeys in the mind.

Where there is despair,
you offer meaningful hope.

Where faith is lacking,
you offer a reason to believe.

Where love has not found a home,
you open the doors of the heart.

When someone needs a friend,
you become a soul mate.

Yes, your words have AMAZING POWER
to help you achieve!

Chapter One

Write Your Book in 90 Days!

We are going to empower you to write your first book in just 90 days, investing only 22 minutes of time per day!

You say you don't believe me?

Well, we both know it can be done. We've done it!

To being completely candid here, you will not finish writing a 300-page *New York Times* best seller in that amount of time. You will not become an instant Sidney Sheldon, Danielle Steele, or Dan Brown. You WILL, however, have written an actual book of 25, 50, 75, or 100 pages or more. The length of your first effort is not important. It's about your decision, desire, dedication, and determination to write, write, and write some more. Furthermore, you will be proud of what you have accomplished. People in your life will want to read it, and they will enjoy it!

What happens to your new baby after that is entirely up to you. Do you want to find a publisher for your work? Do you want to self-publish your book or offer it as an online download—either free or for sale? Do you want to find a literary agent and launch a new career as an author? Only YOU can answer those questions.

Whatever you decide, we will stand behind you! There are several other books in Mark and Steve's Writers Wisdom Series—now or in the future—that will guide you through the myriad aspects of selling, marketing, and even (gulp!) speaking in public about your book.

You have a story to tell . . . ideas to share with the world. Following the plan in this book is your first big step! So start today, and fill in the blanks!

How to Use This Book

- Grab this book, your diary or journal, your computer, a tablet or a few blank sheets of paper, and a pen or pencil. (Crayons are not recommended, unless you are six years old or younger.)
- Find a quiet place—alone—to begin. (A tropical island might be nice, but if you have a regular life, a chair in the backyard or on your deck or patio will work.)
- You might want to play your favorite music in the background. However, Led Zeppelin or Madonna's tunes could prove to be counterproductive.
- Something to sip on while you think and write could help get your creative juices going. (Long Island Iced Tea may be a bit much . . . and counterproductive as well. So we recommend green or white tea sweetened with stevia or agave.)
- Next, as you read the following pages, fill in the blanks. Do not be afraid to make mistakes. Feel free to start over as many times as you like. (That's why we suggest a tablet, extra paper, or your computer.)

When you get to the last page, you will have a writing plan for your book. Follow the plan, write for just 22 minutes every day, and in ninety days, your book or minibook will be born!

First Step: Gather Your Writing Tools

Everything you do in life can be made much easier by having the right tools at your disposal. Here's our list of basic tools that many writers use. You don't necessarily need all of them, but the more you have, the better.

- ☐ A journal.
- ☐ Notepads (Lots of them, in many locations: car, nightstand, desk.)
- ☐ Pencils and pens.
- ☐ Pulse Smartpen. This device automatically captures everything as you write and draw. Go to www.livescribe.com for dealer information.
- ☐ A small tape recorder or digital voice recorder. Some cell phones also have recorders built in, or you can download an app.
- ☐ Extra batteries.
- ☐ Extra tapes for the tape recorder.
- ☐ Transcriber (for tapes: optional).
- ☐ A small flashlight or a pen with a built-in light, kept by your bed.
- ☐ Another journal or notebook, also kept near your bed. Great ideas often come at night!
- ☐ Computer (a laptop is best).
- ☐ A tablet, such as an iPad. This is a relatively inexpensive device that allows you to type on the road, then download your material to your desktop computer.
- ☐ Word processing software (Microsoft Word is the industry standard).

☐ Screenwriting software, if you're writing screenplays (Final Draft 7 is the most used software).

☐ Honest friends who are willing to be your critics.

☐ People willing to proofread for you.

☐ A good editor.

☐ A dictionary (the biggest one you can find).

☐ A thesaurus (in book form, as well as the Visual Thesaurus software program from Thinkmap: visualthesaurus.com, More about that later).

The FANAFI Principle

FANAFI simply means "Find a Need and Fill It." FANAFI is the basic principle behind every successful business—AND every best-selling book.

Authors such as John Grisham, Nora Roberts, Clive Cussler, Stephen King, Danielle Steele, Dean Koontz, and Stephenie Meyer fill the reader's need for adventure, romance, and mystery. They ENTERTAIN the reader.

Other authors, including Dr. Stephen Covey and Suze Orman, fill needs by writing books that INFORM, ENTHUSE, or TEACH.

And, of course, Dr. Norman Vincent Peale and Zig Ziglar are classic examples of authors whose goal is to INSPIRE.

What needs do you want to find and seek to fill?

Fill in the Blanks!

I want to write a book because: _____

_____

_____

_____

The needs I will fill are: _____

_____

_____

_____

The specific topics I will cover in my book are:

1. _____

_____

2. _____

_____

3. _____

_____

4. _____

_____

5. _____

_____

(Use additional space in your notebook as needed.)

The most important topic to me is: _____

_____

_____

The Four Considerations

Of course, your REASONS for writing your book have to be defined very clearly before you begin. At this point, you need to fill in your best responses to what we call *The Four Considerations*.

1. The PURPOSE of my book is to _____

_____

_____

2. The MARKET (or IDEAL READER) for my book is _____

_____

(Begin with the end in mind. Identify the market that will gladly buy what you have to offer them.)

3. My book will HELP THE READER because _____

_____

4. My book is UNIQUE/DIFFERENT because _____

_____

Your responses to these considerations are very important, because they will help keep you focused on WHY you are writing your book, WHOM you are writing it for, and HOW it will make a difference in their lives. Knowing how it will be UNIQUE will help you set it apart from all the other books people are writing right now—all around the world!

We suggest you copy this page and post it in your work area . . . perhaps right above your computer. Refer to it every time you sit down to write, so that you always keep on track.

Your Title Is Everything

Oops! That's not quite right. Your title is MOST of everything. The *subtitle* is the rest of everything!

Your title has to touch the *heart*, and your subtitle has to reach out to the *head*. Emotion causes the reader to want your book, and logic seals the deal.

Your title is your hook. It's what you use to catch your readers and reel them in. So it has to be catchy! If you were writing a book on how to run a successful yard or garage sale, you might title it *Trash to Treasure*.

Your subtitle is your *promise*. Think of it as your contract with your readers. It tells them what your book has to offer to them. Many (but not all) subtitles include the word *How*. For the example above, your subtitle might be *How to Turn the Useless Junk in Your Garage into Your Dream Vacation!*

We suggest that you create several possible titles and subtitles together. After you've brainstormed your original pairs, you can do some mixing and matching. Again, use your notebook or additional paper and keep working on it until you are completely satisfied.

Here's a five-step plan that practically ensures that you will hit on the best title possible:

1. Imagine yourself to be world's best title writer. Vividly visualize and ardently desire that state of mind, and write from that elevated belief.

2. Have a title party. Invite your smartest, wisest, wittiest, and most delightfully fun friends to conceive titles.

3. Meditate on creating a mega best-selling title. Just before falling asleep at night, repeat these words 100 times: *mega best-selling title.*

4. Instruct your higher self to tell you a magnificent title upon arising. Be absolutely ready to capture it on paper, on tape, or your computer. Even the great writer Sidney Sheldon always had 4 x 5 note pads (with *Sidney Sheldon* in red at the top) handy. He kept them everywhere—in his living room, dining room, kitchen, den, library, bedroom, bathroom, office, cars, and jacket pockets—ever ready to record his flashes of luminosity.

5. Correctly or incorrectly, we assume you're spiritual. Pray before commencing the writing process. Get deep in your spirit and have God cowrite with you. God loves to create and help cocreators.

Mark and Jack Canfield sat in Mark's Jacuzzi one night after the original *Chicken Soup for the Soul* became successful, and they wrote 137 titles in one sitting, envisioning a great publishing future for themselves.

Mark met with celebrity Steve Allen, who was dyslexic. Steve always wrote and dictated 8 books at a time. He told Mark, "No one can have writer's block on 8 books simultaneously, so my creative juices are always ignited."

Mark's student and friend Cindy Cashman made *millions* with the title *Everything Men Know about Women*. Great title, but even better yet—the book was nothing more than blank pages. Book buyers laughed all the way to the cash register, and bought it. Cindy sold over ten million.

You're probably wondering why we're emphasizing your need to come up with the title and subtitle so early in the writing process.

The reason is that most writers *write to the title*. The title becomes your compass. It is your true north! Writers use their title on their way to the destination of a finished book. It helps them focus.

Creating the Perfect Title Is Hard Work

Several factors must be combined in order to write, publish, and sell a successful book, whether it is fiction or nonfiction, a printed book or an e-book. Among those factors are:

- Concept
- Content
- Quality of the writing and editing
- Jacket design
- Marketing and distribution, and, of course,
- Title and subtitle

The right title may be one of the biggest challenges you will face in writing your book. We strongly suggest writing *to the title*. This will help you remain focused, and will allow you to weave your key thoughts together around a single, clear, established theme. Here's what we believe:

Your TITLE is your PREMISE.

At its core, what is your book about?

Your SUBTITLE is your PROMISE.

What will the reader gain by reading your book?

A compelling title and subtitle are essential in nonfiction books. But the better known a fiction author is (John Grisham, Danielle Steele, Tom Clancy), the less important the title becomes.

In general, the more points of the Four Considerations you can work into your PREMISE and PROMISE, the more effective they will be in drawing in the ideal buyer. Again, the 4 Cs are:

- PURPOSE
- MARKET
- HELP THE READER
- UNIQUE/DIFFERENT

But avoid shoehorning everything in. You don't want to get too wordy.

Here are some typical examples of PREMISE and PROMISE:

The Four-Hour Work Week: Escape 9–5, Live Anywhere, and Join the New Rich (Timothy Ferriss).

Quiet Strength: The Principles, Practices, and Priorities of a Winning Life (Tony Dungy).

The Seven Habits of Highly Effective People: Powerful Lessons in Personal Change (Stephen R. Covey).

Get a Website

If you haven't already registered and launched a personal author's website (www.YourName.com), do it the minute you are in front of your computer again. In addition, we recommend a website for *every* book you write, even if all you do with that is redirect it to your personal site. (There are many good services for registering your name/URL and serving your site. Among them: GoDaddy.com.)

Let's Get Started!

TITLE _____

SUBTITLE _____

TITLE _____

SUBTITLE _____

TITLE _____

SUBTITLE _____

TITLE _____
SUBTITLE _____

TITLE _____
SUBTITLE _____

TITLE _____
SUBTITLE _____

Whoa! You're not done yet! Keep thinking! (Use additional paper or your computer as needed.)

Test, Test, Test!

Here's a vital next step. Think of the names of 5, 10, 15 or more trusted friends, and show them this list of your five favorite titles and subtitles. Ask them to rate them from 1 to 5 based on what they (your ideal market) would pay: $4, $10, or your ideal price. Ask, "Would you give me $10 for this book?" (Remember, e-books and audiobooks are the future—if not the present—so you can make money on a $6, $8, or $10 book.) You make it in volume, i.e., how many books you sell. Start with a goal of hundreds and keep expanding it until you get into the millions category. Remember, *The Alchemist* sold over 150,000,000 copies. That number should inspire you to greatness.

Ask them if they have any suggestions for improvement, or even new titles. Of course, in order to do this (and have the results mean something), you'll have to give them an overview of what your new book is about, and even share your Four Considerations with them.

And the money winner is: _____

Choose a Literary Style

As you well know, there are several possible approaches to writing a book. Check the one that best fits your intentions. (It's OK to check more than one.)

☐ **First-person narrative.** You are telling a story . . . about your life, your beliefs, your values, using the words *I, me, my, we, us, our.*

☐ **Third-person narrative.** You can still be the central character, but you frame your writing around words such as *he, she, they, him, her, them.*

☐ **Minisubject books** like the 101 books that Mark coauthored with James Skinner and Roice Krueger. They are great sellers, with titles such as *Chronic Profitability, Why Sages Are Sage and Saints Are Saintly,* and *How to Tame the Email Tiger.* They are all available at www.YouPublish.com. And that is where we want you to put your mini-books.

Because of COVID-19 Joel Osteen, the most watched TV minister in history with a mega church in Houston, Texas and friend of Mark's is mastering the high volume sales of mini-books. Joel's newest mini-book is called *Reboot!* That merely means that it can be done. It is also is faster to write and perfect for a screen-driven audience that wants convenient, bite-sized, specific information that they can almost instantly read, digest, think about and apply.

If your minibook is wildly successful, it will inspire you to make it a major book. Or you can combine minibooks. You can also write them as chapters and ultimately aggregate them into a larger book. The possibilities are limited only by your imagination.

☐ **Parable.** You use a simple fictional story to share important truths or principles. Look up Ken Blanchard on amazon.com. He's a master of the business parable. Dr. Blanchard coauthored many supersellers, including *The One-Minute Manager*. Spencer Johnson's hit *Who Moved My Cheese?* is another amazing example.

☐ **Compilations.** You would tell multiple stories to make your point. These stories could come from historical figures or from everyday people. The Chicken Soup for the Soul books are compilations.

☐ **Fact finding.** If you are writing about yourself, this could mean facts about your ancestry. If you are writing about a specific issue, this could be based on extensive research that you would do. Dan Brown, author of *The Da Vinci Code*, is a superlative researcher whose books have sold millions of copies.

☐ **Academic.** This is a step above fact-finding in that you are essentially writing a master's or PhD thesis. That does *not* mean it has to be boring or weighed down with cumbersome words. If, for example, you are interested in the Civil War, you could research and write on *The Impact of Religious Faith on the Opposing Armies*.

☐ **How-to.** If you have an interest, special skill, or hobby on which you have a fresh, creative perspective, you might want to write a how-to book. After all, you're reading one right now! Example: if you're a sailor, you might want to write about using a sextant as a backup to your GPS. If you make jewelry as a hobby, you might offer tips on firing ceramics or making bracelets or necklaces as gifts.

☐ **Poetry.** You're a poet and you know it? Collect your best work and organize it all into a book. Do it by "theme," by period, or by style. DreamingBear Kanaan, a poet from Hawaii, has mastered the fine art of writing heart-capturing love poetry and profitably selling it from the platform.

☐ **Short stories.** Instead of writing a single, continuous narrative (such as the story of your life), you could compile multiple shorter essays. If it's an autobiography, it could include stories on your parents and siblings, your school years, your college, trade school, or military experiences, your marriage, your children, your career, your grandchildren, your retirement interests, and your beliefs and personal values. Of course, where you are in life as you write dictates how much of each topic you can cover.

No matter what you write, you CAN get it published, even if you decide to do it yourself. Today, with the advent of POD (print-on-demand), you can print one book or several copies at a reasonable price—in paperback, oversize "trade paperback," or hardcover. Many companies do POD books, including Amazon.com in Seattle and Ingram (the world's largest book wholesaler—they sell to bookstores) in La Vergne, Tennessee.

Chapter Two

The Essentials of Storytelling

There are six essential elements in storytelling, be it in novels, screenplays, stage plays, news reports, or short stories.

1. **Character.** Who are the people in the story? What do they do or will they do to propel the story forward? (Character development will be discussed shortly.)
2. **Setting.** In what era will the story unfold? (Biblical times, the Civil War, the future?) In what geographic location? (Big city, small town, foreign country?) In what specific settings? (A prison, a university, a church, a family's home, on a ship—or spaceship?)
3. **Story.** What is the genre? (Romance? Action? Mystery? Comedy?) How is the story structured? What events take place? What happens to the characters? What things do they make happen? What relationships exist? What bonds are forged

with other characters? What elements of storytelling technique will be employed?

4. **Conflict.** Without conflict, there is no story. Which characters want *what*? How far are they willing to go to get what they want? Which characters want to prevent that from happening? What strategies and tactics will they use to frustrate the goals of the other characters?

5. **Arc.** What situations change over time? What happens to change them? (This is called the *story arc*.) Which characters will grow? Which ones will remain about the same? Which ones will regress or get worse? (This is called the *character arc*.)

6. **Resolution.** How does the story end? Is everything resolved satisfactorily, or are there loose ends? (Some loose ends are acceptable: that way readers can come up with their own "perfect" ending.) Do the characters achieve their objectives? Is there some logic or plausibility to the ending? Will the reader or audience be satisfied with the outcome? Or will they think the author cheated?

Exercise Your Mind

Find examples from film or literature that illustrate these points. In what ways do these stories do so? What makes these stories unique?

1. _____

_____

2. _____

_____

3. _____

_____

4. _____

_____

5. _____

_____

6. _____

_____

Story and Character Development

The old riddle, "What came first? The chicken or the egg?" certainly applies to the long-standing discussion of story development versus character development. Which comes first? Which is the most important?

The answer is as confusing as the question. But that doesn't mean you can't find the perfect solution for your book.

Here's the answer: *story and character are completely interdependent.* They must be considered together!

You can only create a compelling story when you develop compelling characters.

And you can only create compelling characters when you develop a compelling story.

Etch this in your brain: story and character are INSEPARABLE!

What Is a Story?

In the simplest terms, a story is the telling of an event, or of an imaginary event, in the past, present, or future. It may or may not be told in the order in which the components of the event took place, or could take place. (This is linear versus nonlinear story telling.)

The five components of most stories are:

1. Characters
2. Events
3. Actions
4. Conflict(s)
5. Outcomes

Simpler stories may not include one or more of these components.

CHARACTERS are largely responsible for ACTIONS.

EVENTS propel CHARACTERS to TAKE ACTION.

CHARACTERS may be in CONFLICT initially, or EVENTS or the characters' ACTIONS may lead them into CONFLICT.

OUTCOMES are the result of what happens to the CONFLICT because of the ACTIONS taken by CHARACTERS in response to EVENTS.

Many stories involve an EXCHANGE. We were all raised on stories that were based on a proposed or executed exchange. (The frog said to the princess, "If you kiss me, I will become a handsome prince.")

The Wizard of Oz and the original *Star Wars* illustrate nearly every point in any discussion of great storytelling.

The Four Cornerstones of Character Development

With apologies to Aristotle (*The Poetics*) and Christopher Vogler (*The Writer's Journey*), we offer our own in-depth exploration of character development. (We recommend both books, by the way!)

The four cornerstones of well-defined characters are:

1. **Temperament type.** For more than two thousand years, writers and philosophers have discussed four basic temperaments (natural dispositions) into which all human beings

fall. We refer to them as *Idealists*, *Rationals*, *Guardians*, and *Artisans*, and will discuss their core needs and how their actions, behaviors, and emotions relate to those needs.

2. **Backstory.** How does the character's past impact his or her present life situation? We will discuss heredity, environment, successes, failures, relationships, emotional and physical challenges, and so on. It's important to knowing the character's backstory so completely that you can live out that story in the pages of your novel, screenplay, or business parable.

   A fill-in-the-blanks form will help you accomplish this task more effectively (see page 40).

3. **Compelling desire.** What does each character want, need, or desire? What is driving him or her? And, again, how far is he or she willing to go to attain those desires? What does the protagonist want? What does the antagonist want? What do other characters want (the ally, the mentor, the gatekeeper, etc.?)

4. **Critical flaws.** Everyone has flaws. Some TV preachers seem to be enticed by sexual temptations. Enron executives, Martha Stewart, and various investment bankers are apparently drawn to easy money. Certain people in our military obviously thought it was cool to abuse prisoners in Iraq. Flaws can either destroy the character, or they can ultimately restore the character to a higher plane. It is up to you to best determine how to play out the characters' flaws—all in the best interest of the story. Will the reader continue to dislike the character and his or her flaws, or will the character somehow be redeemed in the mind of the reader?

   "Know them to write them" is an effective approach to character development. More on that later, when you will have the wonderful opportunity to fill in the blanks on every character in your story.

What Is Your Core Concept?

(Read this entire book and come back to this section afterward. Dog-ear the page to return to it.)

My book is about a main character who is a ☐ man, ☐ woman, ☐ child, ☐ talking animal, ☐ creature from outer space, ☐ other: _____, who *desperately wants* _____

_____

_____

My main character (known as the *hero* or *protagonist*) will be confronted by opponents/adversaries/acts of God to try to keep him (or her) from achieving his goal. Among them may be:

☐ Spouse/family _____
☐ Employer/coworkers _____
☐ Money/lack of money _____
☐ Natural disasters _____
☐ Aliens _____
☐ Outlaws/criminals _____
☐ A government agency _____
☐ Other _____

Events and obstacles my main character could encounter might be:

1. _____

_____

2. _____

_____

3. _____

_____

4. _____

_____

5. _____

_____

The ways my main character may try to overcome these obstacles or events are:

1. _____

_____

2. _____

_____

3. _____

_____

4. _____

_____

5. _____

_____

But the obstacles and events may change. The unexpected could happen. Here's how:

1. _____

_____

2. _____

_____

3. _____

_____

4. _____

_____

5. _____

_____

Ultimately, my main character will triumph because:

1. _____

_____

2. _____

_____

3. _____

_____

4. _____

_____

5. _____

_____

Avoid the *Deus ex Machina*

Here's a great definition of *deus ex machina* that we copied from Wikipedia. (We think that's legal; we'll let you know if we get sued.)

> A *deus ex machina* (literally, in Latin, "god from the machine") is a plot device where a previously intractable problem is suddenly and abruptly solved, usually with the contrived introduction of either characters, abilities, or objects not mentioned before within the storyline. It is generally considered to be a poor storytelling technique because it undermines the story's internal logic.

In other words, don't introduce Superman or Wonder Woman in the last chapter and expect them to clean up the story mess that you've created.

Protagonists must solve their problems on their own, or with the help of an ally, or with the help of an enemy, antagonist, or nemesis who turns from the Dark Side of the Force to come to the aid of your protagonist. (Sorry, Mr. Lucas.)

More on Character—Much More

Let's approach the subject of character development in greater depth. Then we'll give you the opportunity to fill in the blanks and define the people who will populate your story.

The First Key to Developing Interesting Characters: Temperament Types

A few years ago, Steve acquired some invaluable information from his friends Scott Blanchard and Dr. Stephanie Rogers that has changed his life. Although this information has been around since ancient Greece, Scott and Stephanie framed it in a way that made it really useful.

Scott and Stephanie took all of the concepts related to the Myers-Briggs Type Indicator (MBTI) and the David Keirsey Personality Profile (www.keirsey.com) and distilled it so that it could be easily applied by writers.

In a nutshell, they explained that there are four basic human temperaments. Each of these temperaments can be defined by the core needs that are their driving forces. Here they are, along with what Scott and Stephanie suggest are their mottos.

1. **Idealists.**
- Meaning and significance.
- Unique identity.

Motto: "All we are saying is, give peace a chance."

2. **Rationals.**
- Self-mastery.
- Knowledge and competence.

Motto: "There's a logical explanation for everything."

3. Guardians.

- Membership and belonging.
- Responsibility and duty.

Motto: "But we've always done it that way."

4. Artisans.

- Freedom to act on impulse.
- Ability to make an impact.

Motto: "*Carpe diem!* Seize the day!"

While these descriptions are obviously abbreviated, you can sense that because people of different temperament types have different core needs, as your characters they would bring different objectives and perspectives to your story.

To gain clearer understanding of the temperaments, we suggest that you read *Please Understand Me II* by David Keirsey. It's a powerful tool for developing believable characters.

The Second Key to Character: Backstory

What happened to the character prior to the beginning of your story or film? What was the character's life like from birth, to childhood, throughout school, and so on?" This information is known as the character's *background story* or *backstory*.

A person born in New York City will have a different backstory than a person born in Midland, Texas.

- Their heritages will be different.
- Their cultures will be different.
- They will have different educational experiences.
- They may come from different religious backgrounds, or from none at all.

- Their parents may be divorced, remarried, or widowed.
- They may have many siblings, or few, or none.
- Some siblings may be adopted; some may have disabilities.

Yet the New Yorker and the Texan will likely share more things in common than they would with someone from the Sudan, Afghanistan, or Pakistan.

It's important that you consider as many of the aspects of your characters' backstories as possible. You do not have to *reveal* the character's entire backstory, but you must *know* it all. You have to know your characters intimately in order to make them believable and bring them to life.

The Third Key to Character: Compelling Desire

Motivation drives a story forward. The key to the motivation of a character is to give that character a strong want. It is usually the wants or desires of your main character or protagonist that are considered first.

Most wants fit into four basic categories:

1. Spiritual
2. Intellectual, psychological, or emotional
3. Physical
4. Self-serving

Of course, under each of those headings there are hundreds of subcategories.

1. Spiritual
    a. Desire for meaning, purpose in life
    b. Desire for life after death, heaven, reincarnation
    c. Desire for wholeness

2. Intellectual, psychological, and emotional
   a. Desire for an education
   b. Desire for love
   c. Desire for family
   d. The need to help others
3. Physical
   a. Need for food, clothing, shelter
   b. Desire for sex
   c. Desire for touch or affection
4. Self-serving
   a. Lust for money
   b. Desire for fame
   c. Craving for power
   d. Pursuit of prestige

MINIPROJECT

In your notebook or on a separate piece of paper, add your thoughts to each of the four lists.

Compelling Desires in Film and Literature

Most storytelling involves protagonists whose compelling desires or wants are at least one level beneath the surface. Many of these desires are actually revealed slowly throughout the story, as the character's backstory is exposed. They include:

1. Right a wrong or provide restitution.
2. Prevent harm.
3. Save the lost, doomed, convicted, or condemned.
4. Escape (from prison, marriages, situations, or jobs).
5. Catch, prosecute, convict, or kill the villain.
6. Romantic or sexual conquest.

7. Attain great wealth, legally or illegally.

8. Revenge.

MINIPROJECT

Think of seven more possible compelling desires, list them below, and match them to stories from film or literature that illustrate them.

1. _____

2. _____

3. _____

4. _____

5. _____

6. _____

7. _____

Here's the Big One: Critical Flaws!

This is where your main character nearly falls apart. This is where he or she becomes vulnerable. Readers love vulnerability, because it makes them feel superior.

Flaws may be a part of the character's past or from his or her belief system.

Flaws result in setbacks and often lead to a point in the dramatic structure (especially in film, but also in fiction) called the *apparent defeat*.

Here are a few of the more obvious ones. Add your ideas to this list.

1. Greed

2. Dishonesty or untruthfulness

3. Selfishness

4. Uncontrolled anger

5. Sexual impropriety or lust

6. False pride, ego
7. Gossip or failure to keep confidences
8. Unfaithfulness
9. Uncontrolled spending
10. Impulsiveness or poor decision making
11. Poor planning; lack of foresight
12. Insensitivity (an unemotional, unfeeling, hard heart)
13. Recklessness; foolhardiness
14. Indiscretion
15. Stinginess (Scrooge)
16. Pretense, or living a falsehood
17. Arrogance
18. Self-doubt
19. Workaholism
20. Laziness
21. Stubbornness; bullheadedness
22. Sloppiness; lack of attention to detail
23. Inconsistency
24. Resistance to change or progress
25. Alcoholism
26. Drug addiction
27. Secret desires
28. Repressed feelings
29. Abuse
30. Fixations or compulsions
31. Irrationality
32. A disability
33. _____
34. _____
35. _____

FLAWS OF OMISSION

Sometimes a flaw is the result of what a character *failed* think about, evaluate, or do. Causes include:

1. Innocence; naivete
2. Too much trust
3. Denial
4. Sense of invulnerability
5. Procrastination
6. Fear of the known
7. Fear of the unknown
8. _____
9. _____
10. _____

Be sure that you don't go overboard when it comes to developing characters' flaws; otherwise your readers may detach themselves emotionally from the characters and their compelling desires. ("A wonderful likable predator-turned-schoolteacher's fatal flaw is that he is addicted to child porn." Lock him up, please!)

Structure

Here's where you get to rub your brain cells together to build interesting (no, make that *compelling*) characters. Set your imagination free! Your characters can be anything you want them to be. The forms on the following pages will help you.

Character Bio 1

Full Name _____ Nickname _____

Born in _____ Resides at/in _____

Sex _____ Age _____ Race _____ Religion _____

Marital Status _____ Spouse's Name _____

Previous Marriages and Outcomes? _____
Name(s) _____

Child One _____

Child Two _____

Additional Children _____

Mother's Name _____ Age _____
☐ Living   ☐ Dead   ☐ Sick   ☐ Institutionalized   ☐ Irrelevant

Father's Name _____ Age _____
☐ Living   ☐ Dead   ☐ Sick   ☐ Institutionalized   ☐ Irrelevant

Older Sibling's Name _____ Age _____
☐ Living   ☐ Dead   ☐ Sick   ☐ Institutionalized   ☐ Irrelevant

Younger Sibling's Name _____ Age _____
☐ Living   ☐ Dead   ☐ Sick   ☐ Institutionalized   ☐ Irrelevant

Other Significant Person _____ Age _____
☐ Living   ☐ Dead   ☐ Sick   ☐ Institutionalized   ☐ Irrelevant

Character's Temperament:
☐ Idealist   ☐ Guardian   ☐ Rational   ☐ Artisan

Character's General Health _____

College/Major _____ Military Service _____

Early Jobs/Pursuits _____

Current Job _____ Desired Job _____

Hobbies/Interests _____ Likes/Dislikes _____

Major Strengths _____ Major Weaknesses _____

FATAL FLAW _____

Character Bio 2

Full Name _____ Nickname _____

Born in _____ Resides at/in _____

Sex _____ Age _____ Race _____ Religion _____

Marital Status _____ Spouse's Name _____

Previous Marriages and Outcomes? _____
Name(s)_____

Child One _____

Child Two _____

Additional Children _____

Mother's Name _____ Age _____
☐ Living ☐ Dead ☐ Sick ☐ Institutionalized ☐ Irrelevant

Father's Name _____ Age _____
☐ Living ☐ Dead ☐ Sick ☐ Institutionalized ☐ Irrelevant

Older Sibling's Name _____ Age _____
☐ Living ☐ Dead ☐ Sick ☐ Institutionalized ☐ Irrelevant

Younger Sibling's Name _____ Age _____
☐ Living ☐ Dead ☐ Sick ☐ Institutionalized ☐ Irrelevant

Other Significant Person _____ Age _____
☐ Living ☐ Dead ☐ Sick ☐ Institutionalized ☐ Irrelevant

Character's Temperament:
☐ Idealist ☐ Guardian ☐ Rational ☐ Artisan

Character's General Health _____

College/Major _____ Military Service _____

Early Jobs/Pursuits _____

Current Job _____ Desired Job _____

Hobbies/Interests _____ Likes/Dislikes _____

Major Strengths _____ Major Weaknesses _____

FATAL FLAW _____

Character Bio 3

Full Name _____ Nickname _____

Born in _____ Resides at/in _____

Sex _____ Age _____ Race _____ Religion _____

Marital Status _____ Spouse's Name _____

Previous Marriages and Outcomes? _____
Name(s) _____

Child One _____

Child Two _____

Additional Children _____

Mother's Name _____ Age _____
☐ Living ☐ Dead ☐ Sick ☐ Institutionalized ☐ Irrelevant

Father's Name _____ Age _____
☐ Living ☐ Dead ☐ Sick ☐ Institutionalized ☐ Irrelevant

Older Sibling's Name _____ Age _____
☐ Living ☐ Dead ☐ Sick ☐ Institutionalized ☐ Irrelevant

Younger Sibling's Name _____ Age _____
☐ Living ☐ Dead ☐ Sick ☐ Institutionalized ☐ Irrelevant

Other Significant Person _____ Age _____
☐ Living ☐ Dead ☐ Sick ☐ Institutionalized ☐ Irrelevant

Character's Temperament:
☐ Idealist ☐ Guardian ☐ Rational ☐ Artisan

Character's General Health _____

College/Major _____ Military Service _____

Early Jobs/Pursuits _____

Current Job _____ Desired Job _____

Hobbies/Interests _____ Likes/Dislikes _____

Major Strengths _____ Major Weaknesses _____

FATAL FLAW _____

Character Bio 4

Full Name _____ Nickname _____

Born in _____ Resides at/in _____

Sex _____ Age _____ Race _____ Religion _____

Marital Status _____ Spouse's Name _____

Previous Marriages and Outcomes? _____
Name(s)_____

Child One _____

Child Two _____

Additional Children _____

Mother's Name _____ Age _____
☐ Living ☐ Dead ☐ Sick ☐ Institutionalized ☐ Irrelevant

Father's Name _____ Age _____
☐ Living ☐ Dead ☐ Sick ☐ Institutionalized ☐ Irrelevant

Older Sibling's Name _____ Age _____
☐ Living ☐ Dead ☐ Sick ☐ Institutionalized ☐ Irrelevant

Younger Sibling's Name _____ Age _____
☐ Living ☐ Dead ☐ Sick ☐ Institutionalized ☐ Irrelevant

Other Significant Person _____ Age _____
☐ Living ☐ Dead ☐ Sick ☐ Institutionalized ☐ Irrelevant

Character's Temperament:
☐ Idealist ☐ Guardian ☐ Rational ☐ Artisan

Character's General Health _____

College/Major _____ Military Service _____

Early Jobs/Pursuits_____

Current Job _____ Desired Job _____

Hobbies/Interests _____ Likes/Dislikes _____

Major Strengths _____ Major Weaknesses _____

FATAL FLAW _____

Character Bio 5

Full Name _____ Nickname _____

Born in _____ Resides at/in _____

Sex _____ Age _____ Race _____ Religion _____

Marital Status _____ Spouse's Name _____

Previous Marriages and Outcomes? _____
Name(s)_____

Child One _____

Child Two _____

Additional Children _____

Mother's Name _____ Age _____
☐ Living ☐ Dead ☐ Sick ☐ Institutionalized ☐ Irrelevant

Father's Name _____ Age _____
☐ Living ☐ Dead ☐ Sick ☐ Institutionalized ☐ Irrelevant

Older Sibling's Name _____ Age _____
☐ Living ☐ Dead ☐ Sick ☐ Institutionalized ☐ Irrelevant

Younger Sibling's Name _____ Age _____
☐ Living ☐ Dead ☐ Sick ☐ Institutionalized ☐ Irrelevant

Other Significant Person _____ Age _____
☐ Living ☐ Dead ☐ Sick ☐ Institutionalized ☐ Irrelevant

Character's Temperament:
☐ Idealist ☐ Guardian ☐ Rational ☐ Artisan

Character's General Health _____

College/Major _____ Military Service _____

Early Jobs/Pursuits _____

Current Job _____ Desired Job _____

Hobbies/Interests _____ Likes/Dislikes _____

Major Strengths _____ Major Weaknesses _____

FATAL FLAW _____

Character Bio 6

Full Name _____ Nickname _____

Born in _____ Resides at/in _____

Sex _____ Age _____ Race _____ Religion _____

Marital Status _____ Spouse's Name _____

Previous Marriages and Outcomes? _____
Name(s)_____

Child One _____

Child Two _____

Additional Children _____

Mother's Name _____ Age _____
☐ Living ☐ Dead ☐ Sick ☐ Institutionalized ☐ Irrelevant

Father's Name _____ Age _____
☐ Living ☐ Dead ☐ Sick ☐ Institutionalized ☐ Irrelevant

Older Sibling's Name _____ Age _____
☐ Living ☐ Dead ☐ Sick ☐ Institutionalized ☐ Irrelevant

Younger Sibling's Name _____ Age _____
☐ Living ☐ Dead ☐ Sick ☐ Institutionalized ☐ Irrelevant

Other Significant Person _____ Age _____
☐ Living ☐ Dead ☐ Sick ☐ Institutionalized ☐ Irrelevant

Character's Temperament:
☐ Idealist ☐ Guardian ☐ Rational ☐ Artisan

Character's General Health _____

College/Major _____ Military Service _____

Early Jobs/Pursuits_____

Current Job _____ Desired Job _____

Hobbies/Interests _____ Likes/Dislikes _____

Major Strengths _____ Major Weaknesses _____

FATAL FLAW _____

Character Bio 7

Full Name _____ Nickname _____

Born in _____ Resides at/in _____

Sex _____ Age _____ Race _____ Religion _____

Marital Status _____ Spouse's Name _____

Previous Marriages and Outcomes? _____
Name(s) _____

Child One _____

Child Two _____

Additional Children _____

Mother's Name _____ Age _____
☐ Living ☐ Dead ☐ Sick ☐ Institutionalized ☐ Irrelevant

Father's Name _____ Age _____
☐ Living ☐ Dead ☐ Sick ☐ Institutionalized ☐ Irrelevant

Older Sibling's Name _____ Age _____
☐ Living ☐ Dead ☐ Sick ☐ Institutionalized ☐ Irrelevant

Younger Sibling's Name _____ Age _____
☐ Living ☐ Dead ☐ Sick ☐ Institutionalized ☐ Irrelevant

Other Significant Person _____ Age _____
☐ Living ☐ Dead ☐ Sick ☐ Institutionalized ☐ Irrelevant

Character's Temperament:
☐ Idealist ☐ Guardian ☐ Rational ☐ Artisan

Character's General Health _____

College/Major _____ Military Service _____

Early Jobs/Pursuits _____

Current Job _____ Desired Job _____

Hobbies/Interests _____ Likes/Dislikes _____

Major Strengths _____ Major Weaknesses _____

FATAL FLAW _____

Character Bio 8

Full Name _____ Nickname _____

Born in _____ Resides at/in _____

Sex _____ Age _____ Race _____ Religion _____

Marital Status _____ Spouse's Name _____

Previous Marriages and Outcomes? _____
Name(s) _____

Child One _____

Child Two _____

Additional Children _____

Mother's Name _____ Age _____
☐ Living ☐ Dead ☐ Sick ☐ Institutionalized ☐ Irrelevant

Father's Name _____ Age _____
☐ Living ☐ Dead ☐ Sick ☐ Institutionalized ☐ Irrelevant

Older Sibling's Name _____ Age _____
☐ Living ☐ Dead ☐ Sick ☐ Institutionalized ☐ Irrelevant

Younger Sibling's Name _____ Age _____
☐ Living ☐ Dead ☐ Sick ☐ Institutionalized ☐ Irrelevant

Other Significant Person _____ Age _____
☐ Living ☐ Dead ☐ Sick ☐ Institutionalized ☐ Irrelevant

Character's Temperament:
☐ Idealist ☐ Guardian ☐ Rational ☐ Artisan

Character's General Health _____

College/Major _____ Military Service _____

Early Jobs/Pursuits _____

Current Job _____ Desired Job _____

Hobbies/Interests _____ Likes/Dislikes _____

Major Strengths _____ Major Weaknesses _____

FATAL FLAW _____

Character Bio 9

Full Name _____ Nickname _____

Born in _____ Resides at/in _____

Sex _____ Age _____ Race _____ Religion _____

Marital Status _____ Spouse's Name _____

Previous Marriages and Outcomes? _____
Name(s)_____

Child One _____

Child Two _____

Additional Children _____

Mother's Name _____ Age _____
☐ Living   ☐ Dead   ☐ Sick   ☐ Institutionalized   ☐ Irrelevant

Father's Name _____ Age _____
☐ Living   ☐ Dead   ☐ Sick   ☐ Institutionalized   ☐ Irrelevant

Older Sibling's Name _____ Age _____
☐ Living   ☐ Dead   ☐ Sick   ☐ Institutionalized   ☐ Irrelevant

Younger Sibling's Name _____ Age _____
☐ Living   ☐ Dead   ☐ Sick   ☐ Institutionalized   ☐ Irrelevant

Other Significant Person _____ Age _____
☐ Living   ☐ Dead   ☐ Sick   ☐ Institutionalized   ☐ Irrelevant

Character's Temperament:
☐ Idealist   ☐ Guardian   ☐ Rational   ☐ Artisan

Character's General Health _____

College/Major _____ Military Service _____

Early Jobs/Pursuits_____

Current Job _____ Desired Job _____

Hobbies/Interests _____ Likes/Dislikes _____

Major Strengths _____ Major Weaknesses _____

FATAL FLAW _____

Character Bio 10

Full Name _____ Nickname _____

Born in _____ Resides at/in _____

Sex _____ Age _____ Race _____ Religion _____

Marital Status _____ Spouse's Name _____

Previous Marriages and Outcomes? _____
Name(s) _____

Child One _____

Child Two _____

Additional Children _____

Mother's Name _____ Age _____
☐ Living ☐ Dead ☐ Sick ☐ Institutionalized ☐ Irrelevant

Father's Name _____ Age _____
☐ Living ☐ Dead ☐ Sick ☐ Institutionalized ☐ Irrelevant

Older Sibling's Name _____ Age _____
☐ Living ☐ Dead ☐ Sick ☐ Institutionalized ☐ Irrelevant

Younger Sibling's Name _____ Age _____
☐ Living ☐ Dead ☐ Sick ☐ Institutionalized ☐ Irrelevant

Other Significant Person _____ Age _____
☐ Living ☐ Dead ☐ Sick ☐ Institutionalized ☐ Irrelevant

Character's Temperament:
☐ Idealist ☐ Guardian ☐ Rational ☐ Artisan

Character's General Health _____

College/Major _____ Military Service _____

Early Jobs/Pursuits _____

Current Job _____ Desired Job _____

Hobbies/Interests _____ Likes/Dislikes _____

Major Strengths _____ Major Weaknesses _____

FATAL FLAW _____

Character Bio #   (you may make copies of this page)

Full Name _____ Nickname _____

Born in _____ Resides at/in _____

Sex _____ Age _____ Race _____ Religion _____

Marital Status _____ Spouse's Name _____

Previous Marriages and Outcomes? _____
Name(s)_____

Child One _____

Child Two _____

Additional Children _____

Mother's Name _____ Age _____
☐ Living   ☐ Dead   ☐ Sick   ☐ Institutionalized   ☐ Irrelevant

Father's Name _____ Age _____
☐ Living   ☐ Dead   ☐ Sick   ☐ Institutionalized   ☐ Irrelevant

Older Sibling's Name _____ Age _____
☐ Living   ☐ Dead   ☐ Sick   ☐ Institutionalized   ☐ Irrelevant

Younger Sibling's Name _____ Age _____
☐ Living   ☐ Dead   ☐ Sick   ☐ Institutionalized   ☐ Irrelevant

Other Significant Person _____ Age _____
☐ Living   ☐ Dead   ☐ Sick   ☐ Institutionalized   ☐ Irrelevant

Character's Temperament:
☐ Idealist   ☐ Guardian   ☐ Rational   ☐ Artisan

Character's General Health _____

College/Major _____ Military Service _____

Early Jobs/Pursuits _____

Current Job _____ Desired Job _____

Hobbies/Interests _____ Likes/Dislikes _____

Major Strengths _____ Major Weaknesses _____

FATAL FLAW _____

Story Development

BASIC FORMS OF CONFLICT

- **Competition: desire for the same goal.** Two individuals, couples or teams work separately toward a goal which only one of them can achieve. (Two guys want the same girl; two NFL teams want the Super Bowl ring; two Olympic athletes want to win the same event.)
- **Cross-purposes.** This is generally conflict about *how* something should be achieved or some goal accomplished.
- **Crossing boundaries.** A character with a good (or evil) desire crosses the line in terms of appropriate or legal behavior and gets in deep trouble as a result.
- **Loss and recovery.** A character loses something (for example, his or her freedom or something of great value) but though the course of events somehow recovers that which was lost.
- **Loss and revenge.** The character never actually recovers what was lost but is able to avenge the loss, usually in an unexpected and dramatic way.
- **Sexual tension.** A character tries to validate his or her worth or self-esteem through sexual conquest. Or the character cheats on a partner, or the object of the character's desires rejects him or her.
- **Power and position.** A person seeks power, fame, or position, and often destroys himself or herself and others in the process.
- **The road home.** The character faces challenges and obstacles in an attempt to reach a desired destination, whether spiritual, emotional, or physical. (Think Disney movies with animals on a journey.)

- **Coming of age.** Also known as *rite of passage*. The character grows from a child into an adult, often as the result of mastering some great challenge.
- **Desire (want) versus time.** A character wants something (or wants to prevent something, such as a disaster) but is running out of time. This is also known as the "ticking time bomb," and as such, is used in film and literature as a device to add suspense either throughout or near the end of the story. (The ticking clock on the nuclear bomb in *Goldfinger*.)

Understanding Power and Control

Characters in a story, whether in film or literature, may attain, and try to maintain, power or control. This power may be used for good purposes or for evil ones. Among the means of control are:

1. Age.
2. Position.
3. Sex.
4. Money.
5. Knowledge, wisdom, or special expertise.
6. Information. Not the same as knowledge or wisdom; may be used in blackmail.
7. Strength.
8. Weaponry.
9. Alliances; allies, partnerships.
10. Taking of hostages.
11. _____
12. _____
13. _____
14. _____
15. _____

MINIPROJECT

Think of five more possibilities, then come up with examples from film or literature to illustrate all of them.

Understanding Conflict

Great literature, meaningful films, well-told stories, and perfectly told truths all involve conflict. A battle. A war.

Some examples:

- Good versus evil (Adam and Eve versus that snake! It's story number 1).
- Age versus youth (*The Graduate?*).
- The underdog versus the favored one.
- Wisdom versus inexperience (*The Karate Kid*).
- Power versus weakness.
- Skill versus incompetence.
- Faith versus unbelief.
- "Home" versus "away."
- Morality versus immorality.
- War versus peace.
- Stress versus tranquility.
- Men versus women.
- Race versus race.
- Team versus team (sports, business, life).
- Love versus hate.
- Angels versus demons.
- Freedom versus slavery.
- Republican versus Democrat.
- Religion versus religion (Catholic-Protestant, Muslim-Jewish, etc.).
- Giving versus greed.

Suggest your own examples in any of these categories, and explain them.

1. _____
2. _____
3. _____
4. _____
5. _____
6. _____
7. _____
8. _____
9. _____
10. _____

The Roles of Characters

Protagonist. This is the character for whom we cheer—the hero or heroine. This individual can have some critical flaws, but we should basically like, or grow to like, this person (for example, Ebenezer Scrooge in *A Christmas Carol*). This character is driven by a want, need, or desire, but faces opposition or obstacles that nearly prevent the goal from being reached. Most protagonists succeed in reaching their objectives and grow to become better beings in the process.

Antagonist or nemesis. The opposition. The obstacle. This individual is often the primary reason that reaching the goal is such a battle for the hero or heroine.

Ally. Both the protagonist and the antagonist can have allies. Sometimes, though, the allies switch sides, which usually makes the story more interesting.

Mentor. Usually this character is a wise older person. Occasionally he or she can be a savvy younger person—even a totally unexpected character. ("A child shall lead them." "Out of the mouths of babes.") This character offers advice or guidance that helps the hero progress toward the goal. Yoda in the *Star Wars* films is a classic example of a mentor.

Threshold guardian or gatekeeper. This character can be a thug, such as a bouncer, bully, or bodyguard, or a secretary who comes between you and your meeting with the boss. This is usually a lesser character, whose authority is generally eventually overridden—to the great satisfaction of the reader or viewer! The role of this character is often to warn the protagonist or the antagonist that the opposition is approaching.

Herald. A messenger offering important information. R2D2 served as a Herald in *Star Wars* by bearing the holographic message from Princess Leia that was delivered to Luke and Obi-Wan Kenobi.

Shapeshifter. The reader or viewer is never quite sure where this character is coming from—whether they are good or evil—because they seem to be one way at one moment and another way at another. They may be fickle or two-faced, or they may simply not know who they are psychologically, emotionally, or spiritually. If you've ever said about someone, "They seemed nice enough on the outside, but once I got to know them," you know a shapeshifter. Nice guy by day, serial killer by night.

Shadow. This character challenges the protagonist without necessarily being the antagonist. In testing the hero, they may actually bring out the best in them. Think about the drill sergeant in *An Officer and a Gentleman,* played by Louis Gossett Jr. His attempts to drive the Richard Gere character out of the Navy's officer training program serve to strengthen the will and character of the young candidate.

Trickster. Even in the moments of heaviest drama, readers and viewers may need moments of comic relief. The Trickster is often the hero's partner or confidante. The *Lethal Weapon* films offer examples of this, as does the *Beverly Hills Cop* series. In the latter, Eddie Murphy is both hero and trickster.

Other characters. Other people populate every story. The best explanation of how all of this comes together to create a great story and propel it forward can be found in *The Writer's Journey,* a book by Christopher Vogler. It is highly recommended for anyone who wants to pursue dramatic writing, whether in literature or film.

MINIPROJECT

Develop a list of characters from your favorite books or movies that illustrate each of these characters, and explain why they fit the definitions.

Suspension of Disbelief

If you've ever gone to a movie and experienced tenseness during a chase scene or in anticipation of a serious crime that is about to take place, or while watching an attempted escape from kidnappers, you already know about suspension of disbelief.

If you've ever read a novel and had tears well up in your eyes when a child dies, or when characters get divorced, or when the protagonist is in a serious accident, you already know about suspension of disbelief.

You also know about it if you've ever been seriously tempted to do what some people in the audience wanted to do—jump up on the stage of an off-Broadway theater in the middle of a performance of the play *Extremities* and beat the pulp out of the villain who was terrorizing the heroine.

Suspension of disbelief simply means that, for a moment in time, you are so drawn into the characters and situations of a movie, a play, or a novel, that you forget that you're watching a movie or play or reading a book.

To achieve this in the work you write, you must:

1. Create believable characters.
2. Get the reader or audience to like the characters, or at least care what happens to them. (Reader and viewers can also suspend disbelief with unlikable characters.)
3. Create believable situations even if they are unbelievable. *Star Wars* is a perfect example of an unbelievable setting that became believable.
4. Keep the moment alive once you have captured it. Don't throw something bizarre and extraneous into the middle of a captivating scene unless you *really* know what you're doing.

MINIPROJECT

Cite some examples of instances when you have suspended your disbelief.

Chapter Three

Let's Get Down to Business

Now it's time to get down to business.

Your Most Difficult Assignment

The next thing on your to-do list is the most difficult challenge you will face in writing your book.

Wait! That's not quite true. We probably shouldn't tell you this, but there is one assignment later on that is even more difficult. But by the time you get to it, you'll be ready for it!

This assignment is to write an overview of what you will put in each chapter, and, after you do, give your chapter a name—other than "chapter 1," of course.

Remember, you will write to your title. It is your compass. Post the Four Considerations above your workspace. They are your roadmap. But now you are going to think about all the left turns, right turns, curves, and straightaways on that map.

You can do this as many times as you want. Use your notebook or your computer, or copy this page so that you can do this over and over and over. You want to get this part right!

One more important note. You do not have to write a linear book. It can be nonlinear. It can be out of order. For example, if you are writing about your life, you can write the introduction about where you are at this point in your life. Then you can go back to elementary school in chapter 1, set up a problem or situation, and then, in chapter 2, explain why or how that problem developed, perhaps because of some prior incident.

Think about movies. They flash forward. They flash back. That heightens interest and keeps the viewer involved,

It's the same with books—whether nonfiction or fiction. You want your book to be a page turner. Dan Brown uses verbs everywhere, spiced up with cliffhanger sequences, so that you have to know what happens next!

Sidney Sheldon was notorious for his chapter endings. His books were universally known as page-turners. His readers often complained to him that he kept them up all night. They'd promise themselves to read just one more chapter, but when they'd get to the end of the chapter, they were so intrigued, they'd have to keep reading. No choice! Playwrights strive for strong "curtain lines" at the end of each scene. TV writers employ the same tactic for the parts just before the commercial breaks. They are very strategically timed.

Let's get started! Copy your title and subtitle from the previous exercise (yes, again!), and move ahead from there.

Use your notebook for additional chapter outlines.

TITLE _____

SUBTITLE _____

INTRODUCTION

This book is about _____

_____,

and here's why my readers should read it: _____

_____

Chapter One

My MAIN point is _____

_____

_____

Here's what I will say to support my main point:

1. _____

_____

2. _____

_____

3. _____

_____

4. _____

_____

5. _____

_____

6. _____

_____

Based on these ideas, the perfect title for this chapter is:

_____

Chapter Two

My MAIN point is _____

_____

_____

Here's what I will say to support my main point:

1. _____

_____

2. _____

_____

3. _____

_____

4. _____

_____

5. _____

_____

6. _____

_____

Based on these ideas, the perfect title for this chapter is:

_____

Chapter Three

My MAIN point is _____
_____
_____

Here's what I will say to support my main point:

1. _____
_____

2. _____
_____

3. _____
_____

4. _____
_____

5. _____
_____

6. _____
_____

Based on these ideas, the perfect title for this chapter is:

_____

Chapter Four

My MAIN point is _____

_____

_____

Here's what I will say to support my main point:

1. _____

_____

2. _____

_____

3. _____

_____

4. _____

_____

5. _____

_____

6. _____

_____

Based on these ideas, the perfect title for this chapter is:

_____

Chapter Five

My MAIN point is _____
_____
_____

Here's what I will say to support my main point:

1. _____
_____

2. _____
_____

3. _____
_____

4. _____
_____

5. _____
_____

6. _____
_____

Based on these ideas, the perfect title for this chapter is:

_____

Chapter Six

My MAIN point is _____

_____

_____

Here's what I will say to support my main point:

1. _____

_____

2. _____

_____

3. _____

_____

4. _____

_____

5. _____

_____

6. _____

_____

Based on these ideas, the perfect title for this chapter is:

_____

Chapter Seven

My MAIN point is _____

_____

_____

Here's what I will say to support my main point:

1. _____

_____

2. _____

_____

3. _____

_____

4. _____

_____

5. _____

_____

6. _____

_____

Based on these ideas, the perfect title for this chapter is:

_____

Chapter Eight

My MAIN point is _____

_____

_____

Here's what I will say to support my main point:

1. _____

_____

2. _____

_____

3. _____

_____

4. _____

_____

5. _____

_____

6. _____

_____

Based on these ideas, the perfect title for this chapter is:

_____

Chapter Nine

My MAIN point is _____

_____

_____

Here's what I will say to support my main point:

1. _____

_____

2. _____

_____

3. _____

_____

4. _____

_____

5. _____

_____

6. _____

_____

Based on these ideas, the perfect title for this chapter is:

_____

Chapter Ten

My MAIN point is _____

_____

_____

Here's what I will say to support my main point:

1. _____

_____

2. _____

_____

3. _____

_____

4. _____

_____

5. _____

_____

6. _____

_____

Based on these ideas, the perfect title for this chapter is:

_____

Chapter Eleven

My MAIN point is _____

_____

_____

Here's what I will say to support my main point:

1. _____

_____

2. _____

_____

3. _____

_____

4. _____

_____

5. _____

_____

6. _____

_____

Based on these ideas, the perfect title for this chapter is:

_____

Chapter Twelve

My MAIN point is _____

_____

_____

Here's what I will say to support my main point:

1. _____

_____

2. _____

_____

3. _____

_____

4. _____

_____

5. _____

_____

6. _____

_____

Based on these ideas, the perfect title for this chapter is:

_____

Chapter Thirteen

My MAIN point is _____

_____

_____

Here's what I will say to support my main point:

1. _____

   _____

2. _____

   _____

3. _____

   _____

4. _____

   _____

5. _____

   _____

6. _____

   _____

Based on these ideas, the perfect title for this chapter is:

_____

Chapter Fourteen

My MAIN point is _____

_____

_____

Here's what I will say to support my main point:

1. _____

_____

2. _____

_____

3. _____

_____

4. _____

_____

5. _____

_____

6. _____

_____

Based on these ideas, the perfect title for this chapter is:

_____

Chapter Fifteen

My MAIN point is _____

_____

_____

Here's what I will say to support my main point:

1. _____

_____

2. _____

_____

3. _____

_____

4. _____

_____

5. _____

_____

6. _____

_____

Based on these ideas, the perfect title for this chapter is:

_____

Chapter Sixteen

My MAIN point is _____

_____

_____

Here's what I will say to support my main point:

1. _____

_____

2. _____

_____

3. _____

_____

4. _____

_____

5. _____

_____

6. _____

_____

Based on these ideas, the perfect title for this chapter is:

_____

Chapter Seventeen

My MAIN point is _____

_____

_____

Here's what I will say to support my main point:

1. _____

_____

2. _____

_____

3. _____

_____

4. _____

_____

5. _____

_____

6. _____

_____

Based on these ideas, the perfect title for this chapter is:

_____

You're Ready to Write!

This is the big moment! You're ready to start writing! No excuses. No delays. You need to start now!

Of course, there are more writing tips to follow. Most of those tips are designed to help you improve what you've started. We certainly don't mean to discourage you, but FIRST drafts are seldom (if ever!) FINAL drafts.

Later on, we will offer you all kinds of tips on editing and rewriting. (It's not as difficult or labor-intensive as it sounds—and you will be pleasantly surprised by the outcome!)

If you want to read ahead, feel free. But don't use reading ahead as an excuse to avoid writing.

Track Your Time

We believe that you can write your book in 90 days by investing just 22 minutes each day. That's why we're asking you to track your time on the charts we've included.

Some words of caution—and encouragement!

Don't punish yourself if you write for *more* than 22 minutes. Don't punish yourself if you write for *fewer* than 22 minutes. We're not here to make you feel guilty. We're not your seventh-grade English teacher. We're not your parents. We're not the writing police. We want you to enjoy this!

The purpose of life, we feel, is the joy of creation. We enjoyed creating this book for you. We want you to thrill to the process the way we do.

The First 30 Days

DATE	TIME	WHAT I DID

Days 31 to 60

DATE	TIME	WHAT I DID

Days 61 to 90

DATE	TIME	WHAT I DID

How Is It Going?

We know what you're doing! You're reading ahead, right? Even if you've only written 22 minutes a day for 12 days, we really don't mind. That's because you'll be able to apply new ideas as you write. Nothing wrong with that! Just remember to write every day . . . and record your dates and numbers of minutes. If you fall short a few minutes, just add it on when you have sufficient time to catch up and especially when you are on-fire with inspiration.

Bonus idea: Remember to program yourself each night saying repetitively before sleep: "Tomorrow I will be thrilled and enjoy writing my best work ever for 22 non-stop minutes!!!"

Honing Your Writing Skills: Tips to Live By
FIND THE RIGHT WORDS

Here are four ways to say the same thing:

Version 1: Work hard to choose the right word.

Version 2: Work diligently to select the perfect word.

Version 3: Strive to find the perfect word.

Version 4: Stuffy version: Passionately pursue the perfect pronoun. (Wow! Alliteration with no point to it!)

Which version would you choose? (We'd go with 3.)

Invest the extra time required to find exactly the right word. Use a thesaurus to search for the shade of meaning that enhances clarity. Write and rewrite until every word is perfectly chosen, and you love it!

We suggest that you purchase Visual Thesaurus (more on that at the end of this book or on our website) and install it on your computer, because it gives you a fast and easy way to find unique and powerful alternatives to your original word choice. Plus it provides the dictionary definitions in a sidebar.

Don't Repeat Words

By that we mean, don't use the same word several times within a few paragraphs unless you are doing so for dramatic or comedic effect.

An example of dramatic effect would be: "He adored her. He adored everything about her. He even adored the things about her that were not especially adorable."

Most great comedians set up the situation or comedic framework by repeating the setup several times. When the punch line is finally delivered, it has maximum comedic effect. Among the best comedians to use this are Bob Hope, Robin Williams, and Stephen Wright.

But here's an example that is not so hot:
Susan followed George through the French doors that opened *directly* into his comfortable study. George *directed* her attention to a framed document on the wall, *directly* behind his desk.

A little better:
Susan followed George through the French doors that opened into his comfortable study. He *called* her attention to a framed document on the wall, *directly* behind his desk.

Best:
Susan followed George through the French doors that opened into his comfortable study. He called her attention to a framed document on the wall behind his desk.

In the third example, repetitive words and been eliminated—as have useless words.

Think and Write in Threes

There is POWER in threes. People can comprehend three points. They can remember three points. They can apply three points.

- Comprehend
- Remember
- Apply

Here are some familiar sets of threes (fill in the blanks):

Father, Son, and _____ _____.

Earth, Wind, and _____.

Rock, paper, and _____.

Veni, vidi, vici: I came, I saw, I _____. (Caesar)

Faith, hope, and _____.

   (And the greatest of these is _____.)

Baseball, apple pie, and _____. (If you're under 40, you may not remember that the last word is *Chevrolet*. Smile!)

Finish the Phrase and Get It Right: Grammar 101

Learn how to do a mental grammar check. The three top secrets are:

1. Finish the sentence.
2. Remove the parenthetical/prepositional phrase.
3. Know what the *real* subject is.

Here's an example of finishing the sentence:

   The original sentence: "He is taller than me."

   What was really said: "He is taller than me am tall."

   Example of the sentence, finished: "He is taller than I am tall."

   Correct abbreviated version: "He is taller than I."

To make it unstuffy and still correct, you might want to write: "I am shorter than he is." (Definitely *not* "I am shorter than him.")

Now an example of both *removing the parenthetical clause* (in this case, it begins with a preposition) and *knowing what the* real *subject is.*

Original: "None of the other guys are going to the game."

Parenthetical clause removed: "None (of the other guys) are going to the game." ("None" is the same as "not one" or "no one," both of which are singular.)

Correct sentence: "None of the other guys is going to the game."

But because the last version (the correct one) sounds stupid, we prefer to reword in cases such as this.

"No one else is going to the game."

"I'm the only one going to the game."

"Not one other guy is going to the game."

Here's another one:

"A guy as valuable as him. . . ."

"A guy as valuable as him is. . . ." NO!

"A guy as valuable as he is. . . ." YES!

But NOT "A guy as valuable as he makes great contributions to the team," because it's stuffy-sounding.

That brings us to an important tip: *If it sounds stupid, rewrite it.*

Bad:

There are a wide variety of techniques available to create the original shapes, such as: slip casting, coiling, hand building, slabbing, assembly, and wheel throwing.

Reworded, but incorrect:

A wide variety of techniques are available to create the original shapes, such as: slip casting, coiling, hand building, slabbing, assembly, and wheel throwing.

Correct but stuffy:

There *is* a wide variety of techniques available to create the original shapes, such as: slip casting, coiling, hand building, slabbing, assembly, and wheel throwing.

Also correct but still stuffy:

A wide variety of techniques *is* available to create the original shapes, such as: slip casting, coiling, hand building, slabbing, assembly, and wheel throwing.

Reworded, correct, and not stuffy:

Many techniques *are* employed to create the original shapes. These methods include slip casting, coiling, hand building, slabbing, assembly, and wheel throwing.

In this case, it's all about matching the number of the noun with the number of the verb. You accomplish this by ignoring, or bracketing, the parenthetical phrase—the phrase that begins with "of," "to," "with," etc.: "a wide variety [of techniques]."

Tip: If you have the opportunity to help preserve the English language without sounding corny or stuffy, please feel free to do so.

And remember this from seventh-grade English class: *There* is NEVER the subject!

Tips and Tricks from the Professionals

1. As a writer, you are not getting paid by the pound. Brevity is a virtue. Use only the number of words or pages needed to accomplish your objectives. (There are exceptions, such as when your editor asks for an article of X number words, or when your book publishing contract specifies a certain length. And publishers do tell you how many words/pages they want you to write.)

2. Sincerity, honesty, and candor will score big points for you as a writer.

3. Humor can be extremely effective, if it is not injected without purpose.

4. Read your work aloud. Lots of bad stuff will magically disappear as a result.

5. Write first, write lots; edit last, edit lots. Your initial writing should be as original as possible: write what you know, and then study and research your subject to become expert.

6. Save every version on your computer. Rename your documents every 5–10 days (with new version numbers) so that you don't lose good ideas from previous versions. True, you may end up with 30 versions of the same manuscript, but hard-drive space is cheap. For even more safety, back up everything on a thumb drive and carry it around with you until your work is published. You can also email your progressive versions to yourself, because your emails are stored on an offsite server.

7. Paste deleted material into a separate document so that you can retrieve it later if necessary.

8. Understand the distinction between academic and popular or commercial writing styles. Academic style is employed in, for example, textbooks and employs a formal style, with no pop-

ular or casual phrases. You will not see slang such as *cool* or *hype* in an academic work. In popular and commercial books, *cool* is cool! Each has its place. Popular and commercial writing is more profitable, widely read, and memorable.

9. Understand shades of meaning ("impaired judgment" versus "diminished judgment.")

10. There is a difference between *who* and *that*: people are *who*; companies and organizations are *that*. Don't write, "I know people that" and "I know companies who . . ."

11. Strunk and White's *The Elements of Style* is the best little book on writing ever! If you don't have a copy, buy one. The original edition is available from Amazon.com for Kindle and iPhone/iPad for under $5.

12. Imagination creates your writing reality. Use you imagination actively to create vivid breakthrough writing.

Use Power Words

Put action in your writing by using power words.

Verbs are power words. Pack your writing with them!

Then enhance the sentence with adjectives and adverbs that help create a more colorful image of what you are telling the reader. We lump adjectives and adverbs together in a single word: *descriptors*.

Here's an example:

Jim ran as fast as he could.

versus:

Jim ran at breakneck speed, his arms flailing wildly.

If we came up with an effective example, you should have a much more vivid mental image of Jim running after reading the second statement. Don't just write it—IGNITE it!

Say It in Fresh Ways

An easy way to add variety to your writing, especially if you are employing dialogue, is to use alternative words for the old standbys *said* and *asked*.

Here are some basic examples. Notice that we've included blank spaces so that you can add your own ideas. Try it! Send your ideas to us. Each month we will award a complete set of Speed books to the person who suggests the greatest number of additional alternatives. (Send your entry to Lila@MarkVictorHansen.com.)

BILL SAID:

Bill acknowledged	Bill hesitated	Bill retorted
Bill added	Bill joked	Bill shouted
Bill admitted	Bill lamented	Bill stammered
Bill agreed	Bill lauded	Bill stated
Bill balked	Bill muttered	Bill submitted
Bill cajoled	Bill noted	Bill suggested
Bill cheered	Bill noticed	Bill teased
Bill chided	Bill observed	Bill yelled
Bill commented	Bill offered	_____
Bill conceded	Bill persisted	_____
Bill confessed	Bill probed	_____
Bill confided	Bill promised	_____
Bill confirmed	Bill proposed	_____
Bill continued	Bill raged	_____
Bill demanded	Bill ranted	_____
Bill exclaimed	Bill reinforced	_____
Bill explained	Bill replied	_____
Bill grumbled	Bill responded	_____

SARAH ASKED:

Asked Sarah   _____   _____

Questioned Sarah   _____   _____

Sarah wondered   _____   _____

Queried Sarah   _____   _____

Puzzled Sarah   _____   _____

Posed Sarah   _____   _____

Pondered Sarah   _____   _____

DESCRIPTION

Bill was stymied   Sarah was puzzled   _____

_____   _____   _____

_____   _____   _____

_____   _____   _____

It's not a *story* unless something *happens*.

It's not a *good* story unless something *interesting* happens.

It's not a *great* story unless something *interesting* and *unexpected* happens—with twists, turns, and switchbacks.

Writing with Power

Here are ten objectives of powerful writing. Keep these guidelines in mind as you progress, and use them to gauge your completed work.

1. **Purpose.** Know *why* you are writing. Let the reader know why. Refer to the Four Considerations. (They do not have to be obvious, but your readers *do* need to know why they should read your work. This is sometimes referred to as the *promise* or the *contract with the reader.*)

2. **Direction.** Stay on track. Use the title as your compass.

3. **Momentum.** Write as though your work is a freight train gaining speed throughout its journey. Build interest throughout.

4. **Clarity.** Make sure readers know exactly what you are saying. Sometimes this is the result of simplicity.

5. **Continuity.** Make sure the flow makes sense. Setup precedes payoff. (We refer to setup/payoff as *SUPO*.)

6. **Accuracy.** Accuracy is multifaceted. Get the facts straight. Use correct English grammar, spelling, and punctuation.

7. **Economy.** Avoid or eliminate needless words.

8. **Freshness.** Find new ways to express your thoughts. Avoid clichés. ("Stay on track" in point 2 above is a classic cliché.)

9. **Involve and Engage.** Capture the attention of your reader and hold it throughout. This is hard work, but you *can* do it!

10. **Satisfy.** Your readers should feel rewarded—intellectually, emotionally, spiritually—for staying with you. Or at least they should agree that they had a good time.

How to Achieve These Objectives

1. **Know your audience.** Demographics: age, sex, marital status, geographical location, heritage, education, career, interests, etc.
2. **Work hard.** Organize your thoughts in a variety of ways until you are happy with your plan. Then dig deeply for the best word or phrase.
3. **Edit.** Make it better every time you read or review it.
4. **Rewrite.** As we said earlier, first drafts are seldom, if ever, final drafts.

Core Principles for Nonfiction Writers

Concept. What is the book about? Will the core ideas hook the reader?

Content. What specific points will you make? What will be the scope of the book? What will be included and what will be excluded?

Clarity. Are the key points clear? Are they in the correct order? Is everything explained adequately?

Flow. Are phrases and sentences as smooth as butter, or are readers likely to get tripped up on clumsy wording? Are the words a pleasure to read?

Writing Books That Sell

For several years, we've been trying to come up with some basic reasons why some books by unknown authors take off while other books, even those by well-known authors, die on the bookstore shelves.

Of course, thoughts such as "fresh," "different," and "unique" come to mind. But many books that fail are fresh, different, and unique.

Then we decided it had to be luck, great marketing, word of mouth, or *Oprah*. We don't really believe in luck, although we do believe in great marketing. As for word of mouth and an appearance on *Oprah*, they have to be earned. In fact, Mark sold more than 12 million books before his first appearance on *Oprah*.

Finally we concluded that it had to be something specific and quantifiable about the writing itself, so we made a list of the ones we could identify. A book does not need all of these characteristics to succeed—but the more the better. Think about the books you love, then tell us if you agree or disagree.

Key Characteristics of a Successful Book

A successful book is:

1. **Substantial.** It presents solid core ideas.
2. **Fanciful.** It often, though not always, presents a whimsical subtext. It may awaken the hero or the champion in the reader.
3. **Factual.** It offers supporting data, interesting stories, illustrations.

4. **Relational.** It connects with the reader on a personal level.
5. **Emotional.** It elicits deeper responses—more than yes or no.
6. **Applicable.** The ideas presented can be clearly understood. They can be either accepted or rejected, depending on the reader's experiences and point of view.
7. **Actionable.** It brings about change through a call for change, personal reflection, or new thinking.

If you successfully combine all of these characteristics, your book will be INTERESTING. No one wants to read a boring, lifeless book. Do you?

Because this is so significant, we're going to ask you to fill in the blanks again—with your responses to these seven points.

1. Why is my book *substantial*? What core ideas am I presenting?

   _____

   _____

   _____

2. What is *fanciful* about my book or the images I create? What inspires the reader's imagination? What awakens the hero that lives within each of us?

   _____

   _____

   _____

3. Am I offering *factual* information? What stories and illustrations do I use to support my ideas?

   _____

   _____

   _____

4. Is my book *relational*? How do I connect with my readers on a personal level?

_____

_____

_____

5. Is my book *emotional*? Am I able to trigger my readers to cry, laugh, fear, or overcome? Am I inspiring them?

_____

_____

_____

6. Are the ideas in my book *applicable*? Will the reader will be able to easily understand and use them for the betterment of his or her daily life?

_____

_____

_____

7. Does my book present something *actionable*? What specific steps can the reader take to create a new paradigm in his or her life?

_____

_____

_____

Editing Your Work

The idea of editing your book may seem intimidating at first. But it isn't all that awful.

Think about it. You've edited your emails. You've edited letters, memos, and reports. Chances are, you've even edited your Facebook page and your text messages.

Editing has often gotten a bad rap. It really means making your writing better—Improving what you've written.

So what are the keys to effective editing, to making it better?

Five points:

- Accuracy
- Organization
- Clarity
- Simplicity
- Rhythm

In terms of *accuracy*, review your facts to make sure they are correct. Look at your spelling, your grammar, and your punctuation. Connect the dots.

When it comes to *organization*, make sure that your readers have everything they need in order to get the flow of what you're saying. Setup always precedes payoff. Again, that does not mean that your story can't be nonlinear. It simply means that you need to wrap up the loose ends before you end your book.

As to *clarity*, make sure that the reader fully understands (and can't misinterpret) what you are saying. That means choosing your words carefully. Read what you write aloud, and you will uncover all sorts of thoughts and ideas that need to be clarified.

Simplicity: Say what you mean, and don't use extra words to say it. Go for the reader's mind, heart, and soul as directly as you can.

Rhythm is somewhat elusive. We believe that it means:
- Is your writing easy to read? Is it as smooth as butter?
- Can you write in a style that prevents readers from tripping over words and phrases?
- Are your words pleasing? Would your friends enjoy listening to your book if it was being read to them?

As you edit, consider these five points above. Watch for problems, spot them, and change them!

In addition to doing your own edit, you may want to obtain the services of a friendly, capable, competent, helpful guide, director, or editor. Most writers set their work aside, let it sit for a day or week, and then edit. Many of your ideas will be edited into this ever-evolving fill-in-the-blank book series.

Rewriting: Painful, but Worth It!

We're doing our best to help you create a book that will convey your core ideas and beliefs to your family, your fiends, and—hopefully—a global audience. And we want you to make some big bucks doing it.

We don't want to discourage you here, but there are best-selling authors—timeless authors—who have rewritten their books dozens of times.

The difference is often between *good* and *great*.

The most important task is to rewrite the first words of every chapter to make them more compelling.

Grabbing Attention: The First Five

It is vital to capture the reader's attention immediately. The best way to do this is through the *First Five Rule*.

Here's how it works.

- Incompetent writers never capture the reader's attention. In some books, the first line of dialogue doesn't appear until page 45. Worse yet, the 44 pages of description in between are horrible.
- Average writers may (or may not) capture the reader's attention in five pages.
- Good writers will likely capture readers in five paragraphs.
- Better writers can hook readers in five sentences.
- The best writers can do it in five words. Dan Brown's first words are always grabbers!

The First Five rule is somewhat flexible. It can be five words, seven words, ten words, four words. At the beginning of *A Tale of Two Cities*, Charles Dickens wrote, "It was the best of times, it was the worst of times." Twelve words, but a great hook.

The first book of the Bible begins with, "In the beginning, God created . . ." What a perfect setup for what life might all be about!

This principle applies to music too. Think about the opening guitar riff of "(I Can't Get No) Satisfaction" by the Rolling Stones. Classic hook!

In his Fifth Symphony, Beethoven hooked us with just four notes: "Dit, dit, dit, DAAAAH!" (Or " . . . _"—Morse code for V, *victory.*)

The more chapters and paragraphs to which you successfully apply the First Five rule, the more likely your readers will remain engaged.

So Let's Do This Now!

Let's take another look at the first draft of the book you've written, along with the first few words of each chapter.

INTRODUCTION

This is how my book is set up. Here is my central point:

_____

_____

Here are my original first five words (or 3–12 words):

_____

_____

Here are my *new* or *improved* five words (or 3–12 words):

_____

_____

Chapter One

My chapter title is: _____

My main point is: _____

_____

Here are my original first five words (or 3–12 words):

_____

_____

Here are my *new or improved* five words (or 3-12 words):

_____

_____

Chapter Two

My chapter title is: _____

My main point is: _____

_____

Here are my original first five words (or 3–12 words):

_____

_____

Here are my *new or improved* five words (or 3-12 words):

_____

_____

Chapter Three

My chapter title is: _____

My main point is: _____

_____

Here are my original first five words (or 3–12 words):

_____

_____

Here are my *new or improved* five words (or 3-12 words):

_____

_____

Chapter Four

My chapter title is: _____

My main point is: _____

_____

Here are my original first five words (or 3–12 words):

_____

_____

Here are my *new or improved* five words (or 3-12 words):

_____

_____

Chapter Five

My chapter title is: _____

My main point is: _____

_____

Here are my original first five words (or 3–12 words):

_____

_____

Here are my *new or improved* five words (or 3-12 words):

_____

_____

Chapter Six

My chapter title is: _____

My main point is: _____

_____

Here are my original first five words (or 3–12 words):

_____

_____

Here are my *new or improved* five words (or 3-12 words):

_____

_____

Chapter Seven

My chapter title is: _____

My main point is: _____

_____

Here are my original first five words (or 3–12 words):

_____

_____

Here are my *new or improved* five words (or 3-12 words):

_____

_____

Chapter Eight

My chapter title is: _____

My main point is: _____

_____

Here are my original first five words (or 3–12 words):

_____

_____

Here are my *new or improved* five words (or 3-12 words):

_____

_____

Chapter Nine

My chapter title is: _____

My main point is: _____

_____

Here are my original first five words (or 3–12 words):

_____

_____

Here are my *new or improved* five words (or 3-12 words):

_____

_____

Chapter Ten

My chapter title is: _____

My main point is: _____

_____

Here are my original first five words (or 3–12 words):

_____

_____

Here are my *new or improved* five words (or 3-12 words):

_____

_____

Chapter Eleven

My chapter title is: _____

My main point is: _____

_____

Here are my original first five words (or 3–12 words):

_____

_____

Here are my *new or improved* five words (or 3-12 words):

_____

_____

Chapter Twelve

My chapter title is: _____

My main point is: _____

_____

Here are my original first five words (or 3–12 words):

_____

_____

Here are my *new or improved* five words (or 3-12 words):

_____

_____

Chapter Thirteen

My chapter title is: _____

My main point is: _____

_____

Here are my original first five words (or 3–12 words):

_____

_____

Here are my *new or improved* five words (or 3-12 words):

_____

_____

Chapter Fourteen

My chapter title is: _____

My main point is: _____

_____

Here are my original first five words (or 3–12 words):

_____

_____

Here are my *new or improved* five words (or 3-12 words):

_____

_____

Chapter Fifteen

My chapter title is: _____

My main point is: _____

_____

Here are my original first five words (or 3–12 words):

_____

_____

Here are my *new or improved* five words (or 3-12 words):

_____

_____

Chapter Sixteen

My chapter title is: _____

My main point is: _____

_____

Here are my original first five words (or 3–12 words):

_____

_____

Here are my *new or improved* five words (or 3-12 words):

_____

_____

Chapter Seventeen

My chapter title is: _____

My main point is: _____

_____

Here are my original first five words (or 3–12 words):

_____

_____

Here are my *new or improved* five words (or 3-12 words):

_____

_____

Use your notebook or computer for additional chapters.

Guess what? You did it! You just finished the assignment that we told you would be more difficult than deciding what belongs in every chapter and then naming the chapters.

That wasn't so bad, was it? In fact, it was downright fun—because what you have written just got better!

Chapter Four

Now That It's Finished

It is now time to move forward—to the next vital step.

Feedback: The Breakfast of Champions

It is time for you to invite friends and family—as well as coworkers and your harshest critics—to read your manuscript and make honest comments. This can be somewhat frightening, of course.

Don't think that we're picking on you, because *many* best-selling authors solicit honest feedback. Naturally, it's only within their very trusted circle of friends and families. But we know from first-hand experience that it is not uncommon for famous authors to show their manuscripts to family and friends for their thoughts and suggestions prior to submission to the publisher.

Every Chicken Soup for the Soul book has been rigorously tested with its specific target market. We wanted to know if likely buyers will actually buy it. We tested the 250 phenomenal stories in *Chicken Soup for the Teenage Soul* with 12,000 age-appropriate kids at Nickelodeon. Could that be at least part of the reason it sold 19 million copies?

To make this process as painless as possible (and to make sure you actually do it), we have provided the feedback form on the next page. You may make as many copies of this as you need to accommodate your group of preview readers.

Copyrighting Your Work

When you write a book or other creative work, you legally own the copyright the moment you create it. However, for clear evidence of your copyright, you will want to send a copy of the manuscript to the Copyright Office at the Library of Congress in Washington, D.C., either on paper or over the Internet, and register it officially. An online submission costs less than a mailed application. (Currently the online fee is $35.)

Your copyright protects your "expression of an idea," but it does not protect the idea itself. Nor does it protect the title. Anyone can use your title for another book, movie, stage play, or article in a publication, unless they are using it for "the intent of creating confusion in the marketplace" and that intent can be demonstrated with success in a court of law.

The only way to protect your title (and possibly your core idea) is to apply for a trademark. This involves lawyers, searches, and other details, and can cost anywhere from $3,000 to $5,000 or more. Then every few years you have to pay more money to renew it. On top of that, you have to defend yourself against any infringement, or your trademark could eventually be declared vacated, void, abandoned, or whatever the legal term of the day is. This procedure isn't cheap, so you need to determine the value of your title.

I VALUE YOUR FEEDBACK!

Dear Friend:

I have just written my first book, and I am turning to my family and friends for honest feedback. My goal is to make this book as useful and meaningful as it can possibly be. Please help me by reading my manuscript and taking a few minutes to complete this form. Then, please send it back to reception@markvictorhansen.com.

Please rate your choices from 1 to 5, with 1 being "poor" or strongly disagree," 3 being "average" or "neither agree nor disagree," and 5 being "excellent" or "strongly agree." Feel free to add your comments.

THE TITLE: 1   2   3   4   5
A better title would be: _____

THE SUBTITLE: 1   2   3   4   5
A better subtitle would be: _____

The book was clearly organized: 1   2   3   4   5
You could organize it better by: _____
_____

I enjoyed the content of the book: 1   2   3   4   5
Something you could add would be: _____
_____

I learned something from the book: 1   2   3   4   5
What I learned was: _____
_____
_____

I would recommend this book to others: 1   2   3   4   5
If I were writing an ad or endorsement for this book, I would say:
_____
_____
_____

For more information on copyrights, or to download forms or upload your manuscript, go to: www.copyright.gov.

Getting That Silly Bar Code

If you are publishing your book yourself and intend to sell your book through retail outlets, you will need to obtain a computer file (usually a JPEG) of the bar code you see on the back cover of books. This is called an EAN/ISBN number. (EAN stands for European Article Number, and ISBN stands for International Standard Book Number.) This bar code tells booksellers where they need to go to order the book. Your book designer can easily add the bar code to the back cover. (Bar codes are not needed on many forms of e-books or books distributed in PDF format.) For information, go to R. R. Bowker Company at www.bowker.com.

This company also offers a service called "Books in Print." It is a database of all books that are currently available. If you self-publish, you will want to make sure that your book is listed. Information is available at www.myindentifiers.com.

Publishing Your Book

When most people think of publishing a book, the names of major publishers come to mind: Random House, Penguin, McGraw-Hill, Doubleday, Harper Collins, and more.

But in today's Internet-interfaced world, there are many other options for getting published!

Online: Youpublish.com: They enable you to publish your creative works—text, audio, or video—free or for sale. You determine the value of your work. They collect the payment, retain 50 percent, and send you the remaining 50 percent.

Self-publishing: createspace.com.

Print-on-demand: You'll find multiple choices simply by typing "print-on-demand" into a search engine such as Google.

Apple iPad/iPhone: The iTunes online store has created tremendous opportunities for creators of music, videos, e-books, and audio books.

Amazon.com: Amazon now sells more e-books for the Kindle than they do hardcover or trade paperback books. This is a huge market for you!

Promoting Your Book

Before you read another word, we suggest that you register your domain name for your website. *Every* book you write should have its own unique URL and website.

Because there are millions of names already registered (even if they are not actively in use), you may not be able to register your top choice.

Remember, you may be able to register ".org" or ".info" if ".com" is already in use.

List some of your ideas here or on your computer:

www._____._____

www._____._____

www._____._____

www._____._____

www._____._____

Several companies can help you register your domain name. Among the many choices are www.GoDaddy.com, www.Frugal Domains.com, www.Register.com, and www.Web.com. These companies can also host your website.

Other Promotional Tips

You'll earn bonus points from us if you write your own back cover copy for your book. Choose the words that would make YOU want to buy your own book. Write several different versions and test, test, test! Take a look at what other bestselling authors do . . . and top them!

Be sure to read three other books in this series that will help you publish and promote your book. (Some titles may not yet be available at the time you read this book.)

Speed Publish Your New Book
Speed Market Your New Book
Speed Write and Deliver Your Killer Speech

Software Resources

These are our software recommendations:

MICROSOFT WORD

This word processing program is preferred by practically all publishers. It can be purchased bundled with Microsoft Office for both PC and Mac. (Prices vary. Available at www.microsoft.com and retail stores everywhere.)

DRAGON

Speech recognition software (much like Siri) that speeds up getting words on paper. This voice dictation program turns your recorded words into printed words. We have not tried it, but we know writers who love it. A variety of Dragon packages are available through Nuance, at www.nuance.com/dragon.html, for areas such as education, law, law enforcement, financial services, healthcare, small business, and social services.

EVERNOTE

This is a perfect brainstorming and organizational tool that helps you pull together relevant project material from diverse sources, including web searches. Available for download free on the App Store, Google Play, or from Microsoft.

FINAL DRAFT 11

This is *the* essential program for screenwriters, television writers, and playwrights. It formats works according to the industry standard. If you're using an alternative, such as Scrivener (see below), make sure that it translates to Final Draft. There is also an iPhone version that allows you to work wherever brilliant ideas come to mind. It is called Final Draft Mobile, and it is available on the App Store.

SCRIVENER

This writing software (currently for Mac, but in beta form for PC) can help you create e-books for Apple iPad, Amazon Kindle, and other e-book formats. You can also use it to write screenplays for conversion to Final Draft. (See more information in our book *Speed Write Your First Screenplay*.)

HANX WRITER

Created by actor Tom Hanks, this program for smartphones and tablets is just for fun. The screen looks like an old typewriter, and it makes old typewriter sounds. The inexpensive upgrade is worth it. Available on the App Store for free, with In-App Purchases.

INSPIRATION MAPS

This easy-to-use mind-mapping software helps you prepare outlines. It's a great way to organize your thoughts! Don't let the fact that it was designed for K-12 education fool you. It is a powerful program, and less expensive than most. www.inspiration.com/Inspiration.

VISUAL THESAURUS

The Visual Thesaurus from ThinkMap (visualthesaurus.com) is an interactive dictionary and thesaurus. It enables you to search for alternative words rapidly and thoroughly by creating word maps that branch to related words. Say you have a word in mind, like "solid." The VT helps you find words that are both synonyms and antonyms, such as upstanding and strong, or liquid and gaseous, as well as tangential, such as matter and massive. It also supplies definitions and example sentences.

This site will help you to:
- find the right word and discover related meanings
- develop a better vocabulary
- improve your grammar
- master word usage
- check your spelling

SMARTPEN

This pen has a built-in audio recorder that syncs with the words you write on the pages of a special notebook.

Book Proposal Guides

If you want your work to be published by a major publishing house (yes, they call themselves "houses"), you may have to prepare a formal book proposal. This is a kind of extended outline of your book, chapter by chapter, and usually includes a sample chapter and biographical background about you as the author.

Michael Hyatt, former chairman of Thomas Nelson Publishers (the seventh-largest trade book publisher in the U.S.), has written two essential books available as PDF downloads:

Writing a Winning Fiction Book Proposal
Writing a Winning Nonfiction Book Proposal

Michael has also written a book on making your voice heard in a communication-overloaded world. It is titled *Platform: Get Noticed in a Noisy World*.

Additional Resources

Depending on your writing focus (fiction, nonfiction, short stories, screenplays), you will find certain books on this list to be helpful, if not essential. While you may find most of these books in a public library, we strongly recommend that you own these titles followed by an asterisk (*).

THE ENGLISH LANGUAGE

The Merriam-Webster Dictionary* (Merriam-Webster). Use the thickest one available. The standard for most uses is *Merriam-Webster's Collegiate Dictionary*, eleventh edition. Although you can find access to the dictionary online, it is recommended to have a physical copy of the book, because the definitions will often encompass additional meanings you may not find online.

Roget's Thesaurus, eighth edition. Multiple versions can be helpful. Merriam-Webster also offers a thesaurus. Thesaurus.com is also a resource.

The Elements of Style*, by William Strunk and E. B. White (Spectrum, 2018). The classic edition of 2018, edited by Richard De A'Morelli, contains the original version, as well as numerous additions.

The Chicago Manual of Style*, seventeenth edition (University of Chicago Press, 2017). An online version of this text is also available through www.chicagomanualofstyle.org/home.html.

The New York Times Manual of Style and Usage, fifth edition (Three Rivers Press, 2015).

Grammatically Correct, by Anne Stilman, second edition (Writer's Digest Books, 2010).

Elements of Style for Screenwriters, by Paul Argentini, first edition (Lone Eagle, 1998).

The Associated Press Stylebook 2020 and Briefing on Media Law, revised edition (Basic Books, 2020).

CREATIVITY AND STORY

The Writer's Journey, by Christopher Vogler, third edition (Michael Wiese Productions, 2007).

The Poetics, by Aristotle. Various editions.

The Art of Dramatic Writing, by Lajos Egri (BN Publishing, 2009).

How to Write a Damn Good Novel, by James N. Frey, first edition (St. Martin's Press, 1987).

How to Write a Damn Good Novel II: Advanced Techniques, by James N. Frey, first edition (St. Martin's Press, 1994).

SCREENWRITING

Story: Substance, Structure, and the Principles of Screenwriting, by Robert McKee, first edition (HarperCollins, 2010).

Lew Hunter's Screenwriting 434, by Lew Hunter, revised edition (TarcherPerigee, 2004).

Writing Screenplays That Sell, by Michael Hauge, anniversary edition (Collins Reference, 2011).

Essentials of Screenwriting: The Art, Craft, and Business of Film and Television Writing, by Richard Walter, revised edition (Plume, 2010)

Write: Treatments To Sell: Create and Market Your Story to the TV and Motion Picture Industry, by Kenneth Atchity and Chi-Li Wong, second edition (Holt Paperbacks, 2003).

LINDA SEGER'S BOOKS

Making a Good Script Great, third edition (Silman-James, 2010).

Creating Unforgettable Characters, first edition (Holt Paperbacks, 1990).

Advanced Screenwriting: Raising Your Script to the Academy Award Level (Silman-James, 2003).

The Art of Adaptation: Turning Fact and Fiction into Film, first edition (Holt Paperbacks, 1992).

SYD FIELD'S BOOKS

Syd was among the first to explain how it's done.

Screenplay: The Foundations of Screenwriting, revised edition (Delta, 2005).

The Screenwriter's Workbook, revised edition (Delta, 2006).

The Screenwriter's Problem Solver: How to Recognize, Identify, and Define Screenwriting Problems (Delta, 1998).

WRITERS' RESOURCES

These guides to writers' markets are updated annually.

The Writer's Market (Writer's Digest Books). This listing of over 8,000 book and magazine editors includes a partial listing of agents.

Get a Literary Agent, by Chuck Sambuchino (Writer's Digest Books). This is the best book we have ever found about agents and what they seek in authors.

Guide to Literary Agents (Writer's Digest Books). The most trusted guide to getting an agent.

Children's Writer's and Illustrator's Market (Writer's Digest Books).

Poet's Market (Writer's Digest Books).

Novel and Short Story Writer's Market (Writer's Digest Books).

INTERESTING OTHER RESOURCES

Every book of famous quotations you can find. (Internet searches OK.)

Platform: Get Noticed in a Noisy World, by Michael Hyatt, first edition (HarperCollins Leadership, 2012).

A Dictionary of American Idioms, by Adam Makkai, M.T. Boatner, and J. E. Gates, fifth edition (Barron's Idioms, 2013).

Dictionary of Theories, by Jennifer Bothamley (Gale Research, 2002).

The Book of Positive Quotations, edited by John Cook, second edition (Fairview Press, 2007).

Online and Related Resources

ISBN NUMBERS

www.isbn.org. This is the site for R. R. Bowker, the only official place to get ISBN numbers, without paying a needless fee to an "expert" or vendor. (You can also easily find ISBNs on Amazon, and then verify them here.)

COPYRIGHTS

www.copyright.gov/forms. This is where you go to apply for copyrights. You do NOT need a lawyer or some phony "fee-added" vendor to copyright your work. (This is a very slow process . . . electronic filing is a bit faster.)

WRITERS GUILD OF AMERICA WEST

www.wgawregistry.org. This is the place to register your screenplay, treatment, or ideas. Quick turnaround.

WRITER'S DIGEST

www.writersdigest.com. It's a magazine and a website. It publishes books (such as *The Writer's Market* and *Guide to Literary Agents*) and offers classes, teleseminars, and webinars. Get on their email list, then pick and choose what you need.

WRITER'S STORE

www.writersstore.com. All sorts of things for writers: books, software, script covers, *Script* magazine, brass brads (for screenplays), and more.

BRYAN GARNER

www.lawprose.org/lawprose-blog. This sounds as though it is for lawyers, but it's for all writers. It helps with correct usage. You can subscribe to daily usage tips. "Distinctive uses of variations of words" are his specialty.

Ordering information for all these books, as well as for all products mentioned above, is available on our website: www.SpeedWriting Books.com.

Acknowledgments

Thanks from Mark to Crystal, Melanie, and the entire Mark Victor Hansen team. You all get amazing things done!

Thanks from Steve to Mark and the "group," to Karla and his kids, and to the late Ole Loing, his seventh-grade English teacher and encourager.

Acknowledgements

About the Authors

Mark Victor Hansen

Mark is widely known as an American inspirational and motivational speaker, trainer, author, serial entrepreneur, and member of multiple boards of directors. He is best known as the founder and cocreator (with Jack Canfield) of the Chicken Soup for the Soul book series, with more than 500 million copies sold.

For more than forty-four years, he has focused solely on helping people and organizations reshape their personal vision of what's possible. His powerful messages of possibility, opportunity, and action have helped create startling and powerful change in thousands of organizations and millions of individuals worldwide.

With his open, honest, endearing, and charismatic style, Mark captures his audience's attention as well as their hearts. With his one-of-a-kind technique and masterful storytelling ability, he is one of the most dynamic and compelling speakers of our time.

The Chicken Soup idea was just one of many that have propelled Mark into the worldwide spotlight as a sought-after keynote speaker, best-selling author, futurist, business leader, and marketing maven. *Ask! The Bridge for Your Dreams to Your Destiny* was published in 2020. Mark believes it has lightning in a bottle and it will outsell even the Chicken Soup for the Soul series.

The author of many books such as *One Minute Millionaire, Cracking the Millionaire Code, Cash in a Flash, The Richest Kids in America, How to Make the Rest of Your Life the Best of Your Life, The Master Motivator, The Power of Focus, The Aladdin Factor, Dare to Win, The Miracle of Tithing*, and others. Mark has an extensive library of audio programs, video programs, and enriching articles in the areas of "big thinking," sales performance, marketing, publishing, and personal and professional development.

Mark's energy and exuberance travel still further through mediums such as television (*Oprah*, CNN, and *The Today Show*), print (*Time, U.S. News & World Report, USA Today, The New York Times*, and *Entrepreneur*) and countless radio and newspaper interviews as he assures everyone of the inherent genius in all of us if we choose to access our centers of influence, leverage our strengths, and take action.

Mark is the founder of MEGA Book Marketing University, MEGA Speaking Empire, and MEGA Marketing Magic. Each of these annual conferences speaks to the specific needs of those who want to discover, create, and launch business empires. Mark is now doing these as online classes, please visit markvictorhansen.com.

A passionate philanthropist and humanitarian, Mark teaches the principles of the four types of tithing: thinking, time, talent, and treasures. Favored charities are Horatio Alger Scholarships, Habitat for Humanity, American Red Cross, Operation Smile, OCEANA, the Wyland Foundation, March of Dimes, and Covenant House. He is currently cochairman (with his beloved wife, Crystal) of Childhelp Global Fundraising Campaign.

In 2000, The Horatio Alger Association of Distinguished Americans honored Mark with the prestigious Horatio Alger Award. Each year, this association honors American leaders who personify the virtues and principles inherent in the success stories written by nineteenth-century American author Horatio Alger Jr.

As an award winner, Mark Victor Hansen's extraordinary life achievements stand as a powerful example that the free enterprise system still offers opportunity to all.

In 2004, Mark was inducted into the Sales & Marketing Executive International's Hall of Fame, receiving the Ambassador of Free Enterprise award. He is also the recipient of the 2004 Visionary Philanthropist for Youth Award by Covenant House of California.

In 2000, Northwood University honored him as the Outstanding Business Leader of the Year. In 2002, the University of Toledo presented Mark with an honorary PhD in business administration and established the Mark Victor Hansen Entrepreneurial Excellence Fund, which will help shape the minds of future business leaders and assist in the development of the faculty who will teach them. Additionally, Mark has ten honorary doctorates.

Mark presents fifty seminars each year and serves as chairman of Mark Victor Hansen & Associates, Inc. He is cofounder and chief visionary officer of Chicken Soup for the Soul Enterprises, Inc. and is the president of One Minute Millionaire, LLC.

Mark is an enthusiastic crusader for what's possible and is driven to make the world a better place. Currently he and his wife are immersed in their new venture, which is designed to bring affordable, renewable energy and innovative devices to the United States—and the world (www.metamorphosisenergy.us). Watch an informative video at: www.naturalpowerconcepts.com. Their massive transformative purpose: *energy and water independence for everyone, everywhere.*

MARK VICTOR HANSEN QUOTES

May these quotes inspire you to be rich on the inside so that you live the life of your dreams.

1. The size of my asking determines the size of my result.
2. Every time you get rejected, say, "Next."
3. When you know clearly what you want, you'll wake up every morning excited about life.
4. Turn your troubles into treasures. Learn from them and grow from them.
5. You control your future, your destiny. What you think about comes about. By recording your dreams and goals on paper, you set in motion the process of becoming the person you most want to be. Put your future in good hands—your own.
6. For the next thirty days, think, talk, act, walk, smell, and feel like a business is booming, and it will.
7. Miracles never cease to amaze me. I expect them, but their consistent arrival is always delightful to experience.
8. Money never starts an idea: it's the idea that starts the money.

Steve Gottry

Steve Gottry is the founder and president of Gottry Communications Group, Inc., a full-service advertising agency, and Corporate Channels, a video production firm. Both were based in Bloomington, Minnesota, a Twin Cities suburb. He formed the company in 1970 and served a variety of organizations  across the nation. Among his clients were HarperSanFrancisco, Career Press, Zondervan Publishing House, Prudential Commercial Real Estate, Warner Bros., United Properties, World Wide Pictures, NewTek, Inc., and Standard Publishing.

His firm was the winner of a number of national awards, including three Silver Microphones for radio and an award for direct mail from the International Advertising Festival of New York.

His agency was named Small Company of the Year by the Bloomington, Minnesota Chamber of Commerce. Steve was subsequently recognized as the Small Business Advocate of the Year by the chamber.

Steve and his wife, Karla, moved their family to Arizona in 1996, to leave the colder climate of Minnesota in order to enjoy 320 days of warm sunshine every year. He teamed up with Ken Blanchard in October 1998, to collaborate on a number of publishing projects and has since developed writing relationships with several other best-selling authors.

In 2004, Steve was named writer-in-residence at Grand Canyon University in Phoenix, where he taught a class called "Writing as a Career." He is a current member and past president of Dobson

Ranch Toastmasters. A man of many interests, he is an instrument-rated pilot, an avid semipro photographer, and a devoted Arizona Diamondbacks and Arizona State University football fan. He loves the outdoors and prefers to write at a remote campsite, near the ocean, in beautiful Sedona, or simply out by the pool.

Steve is the author of *Common Sense Business* (HarperCollins, 2005), coauthor (with Ken Blanchard) of *The On-Time, On-Target Manager* (William Morrow, 2004), and coauthor (with Linda Jensvold Bauer) of *A Kick in the Rear* (Priority Multimedia Group 2005). He also authored the original "fill in the blanks" book, *The Screenwriter's Story Planning Guide*, which he and Mark have updated and repackaged as *Speed Write Your First Screenplay*.

For many years, Steve and his team did marketing, theater posters, and broadcast commercials for several major motion pictures, including *The Hiding Place*, *Joni*, Johnny Cash's *The Gospel Road*, *Chariots of Fire*, Clint Eastwood's *Pale Rider*, and *Jesus*.

He has written or cowritten the screenplays for four produced television and video/DVD projects, including the script for *The Story of Jesus for Children* (now in 161 languages and viewed by nearly 1 billion people worldwide) as well as *Jacob's Gift* (based on the best-selling book by Max Lucado) and two episodes of *Wondrous Myths and Legends* (Sony Wonder). He also writes, produces, and directs commercial and industrial video projects, and recently won the Aegis Award of Excellence for a pro bono video he created on behalf of UMOM New Day Centers, a group of homeless shelters in Phoenix.

As a ghostwriter, he collaborated with Dr. Ken Blanchard (and the late S. Truett Cathy, founder of Chick-fil-A) on *The Generosity Factor* (Zondervan 2002), and *Zap the Gaps!* (William Morrow, 2002), among others. He did a major edit of Michael Gerber's bestselling HarperCollins release *Awakening the Entrepreneur Within* and contributed to a significant revision of Gerber's book, *The E-myth Enterprise* (HarperCollins, 2009). He recently ghosted *Life through Rosey-Colored Glasses* for NFL legend Rosey Grier.

Steve's website is www.SteveGottry.com.

CPSIA information can be obtained
at www.ICGtesting.com
Printed in the USA
JSHW040440251021
19816JS00003B/4

9 781722 503291